60p
6/24

GW00384795

Schumann

The Great Composers

Schumann

Alan Walker

FABER AND FABER 3 QUEEN SQUARE LONDON

First published in 1976
by Faber and Faber Limited
3 Queen Square London WC1
Printed in Great Britain by
The University Printing House, Cambridge

ISBN 0 571 10269 7

Also by Alan Walker
A Study in Musical Analysis
An Anatomy of Musical Criticism
Franz Liszt (Great Composer Series)

(ed.) Frédéric Chopin: profiles of the Man and the Musician
(ed.) Franz Liszt: the Man and his Music
(ed.) Robert Schumann: the Man and his Music

Contents

Illustrations

*The illustrations on pp. 17, 22, 25, 39, 43, 50, 103 and 115 are reproduced
by kind permission of Robert-Schumann-Haus, Zwickau.*

Music Examples

Childhood and Youth

I

It was 1812. Europe was ravaged by war. Napoleon was at the pinnacle of his career. His troops had smashed the smaller German states to their knees, and were now spreading like a dark stain across the map of the world. Only England and Russia remained. Napoleon decided to settle with Russia first. He raised a *Grande Armée* of half a million men and marched east. His route led him directly through the small town of Zwickau in Saxony. This peaceful community suddenly found itself on the crossroads of Europe. For two days the inhabitants heard nothing but the tramping of feet, the clatter of hooves, and the rolling of drums, as column after endless column of soldiers moved through, finally disappearing across the horizon. Napoleon took Moscow in September 1812. The Russians then burned the city, making it impossible for him to establish winter quarters there. The shattered remnants of the *Grande Armée* now began their epic thousand-mile trek across Europe, back to France. Only fifty thousand men survived the nightmare journey. Some died of hunger; others died of their wounds; many froze to death in the bitter cold. Once again, their route led them through Zwickau. The survivors started to arrive in the spring of 1813. Starving soldiers looted the town for food, leaving disease and famine in their wake. Hundreds of wounded crammed Zwickau's tiny hospitals. Severed arms and legs were piled in the streets outside. The weather was hot and the stench became unbearable. Cholera broke out. A prosperous community of four thousand people lost nearly five hundred of its citizens within a few weeks.

Standing in Zwickau's main square was an imposing house. Napoleon's troops must have marched right past it. If so, they could hardly have failed to notice a large sign saying 'Schumann: bookseller and publisher'. This was the home of August Schumann who lived there

Schumann's birthplace in Zwickau

with his wife, five children and several thousand books. The youngest child, Robert, was only three years old. Like the rest of the family, the boy would have been a witness to some dreadful scenes in the streets outside. Certainly, he would have heard the ominous roll of gunfire while the battle of Leipzig was raging just forty miles away. These were troubled times, and the Schumann family were lucky to emerge unscathed.

From the start, August Schumann had wanted to be in publishing. He had an insatiable appetite for books. By the time he was twenty-one he had written novels and plays, and had amassed a large library of four thousand volumes at great personal sacrifice. In 1795, aged twenty-two, he met and married Johanna Schnabel, the daughter of his landlord, a well-to-do municipal surgeon at Zeitz. Johanna's father thought his daughter's marriage to August beneath her station, for at first he favoured a wealthier suitor. He consented to the match only after the young couple had agreed to go into the grocery business to raise capital. They moved to Ronneburg, a small town in Saxony, and stuck it out for four years. The enterprise foundered, and August, risking everything on his interest in publishing, opened his own bookshop in 1799. The move to Zwickau came in 1808. It was a larger town and possessed a grammar school, which created a demand for books. He quickly established a reputation as a 'scholarly' publisher, bringing out pocket editions of the classics. Soon August had become one of the most respected and influential citizens in Zwickau. There were five children of the marriage, four sons and a daughter. Robert Alexander Schumann was the youngest. He was born in Zwickau on 8 June 1810.

By the time Robert had reached school age the Schumanns were comfortably off and they could contemplate having him privately educated. Of all the great composers, with the exception of Mendelssohn, Schumann probably started life with the best material advantages. At first he had a resident tutor. Later, when he was six years old, he was placed in a private preparatory school run by Archdeacon Döhner. He made excellent progress and remained there for four years. At Easter 1820 he was enrolled into the Zwickau Lyceum. Although the Lyceum specialized in classics, it also offered its students an opportunity for music-making. On its staff was the local organist Johann Gottfried Kuntzsch. He gave the young Schumann his first piano lessons. It is doubtful whether Kuntzsch's instruction amounted to much more than correcting the boy's fingering and guiding him through the simpler works in the piano repertory. His chief importance to Robert was to help him release the powerful musical impulses gathering within him. In later life, Schumann always spoke of Kuntzsch with affection. He once wrote to his old master: 'You were the only one who recognized my musical talent, and indicated the path along which, sooner or later, my good genius was to guide me.' Kuntzsch died in 1855, aged eighty, having spent most of his professional life in Zwickau. It gave him immense pleasure when, in his seventy-seventh year, his fellow citizens presented him with the freedom of the city in recognition of his services. Kuntzsch was busy with music to the end. His landlady returned one night from the theatre and found him dead at his writing-desk, the ink still wet on his pen.

Robert's talent for music was soon spotted by his father. To show his approval, he purchased an expensive Streicher grand piano for his son. Four-handed piano arrangements of the classics now became a regular feature of the Schumann household. Together with a boyhood friend, Friedrich Piltzing, who was also a pupil of Kuntzsch, Robert started to explore the symphonies of Haydn, Mozart and Beethoven. Other players would occasionally be brought in, the young *maestro* directing the ensemble from the keyboard. Sometimes one of Robert's own pieces would be played, much to the delight of August Schumann, who was usually the sole member of the audience. The boy's earliest composition, a set of dances, dates from his eighth year. The most ambitious work of his youth seems to have been a setting of the 150th Psalm for voices and instruments. Most of Schumann's juvenile works have been lost.

Schumann took part in several school concerts while at the Lyceum. He once played Moscheles's 'Alexander March' Variations, a difficult piece requiring a good deal of agility. Passages like the following pose a challenge, and if the boy tackled them successfully we have to acknowledge that his later ambition to become a virtuoso pianist was not based on a mere whim, but on serious accomplishment.

Variation 5

Schumann's parents, 1810

Moscheles, in fact, was one of Robert's early models. In the summer of 1819, the nine-year-old Schumann had accompanied his father to Carlsbad where he had attended a recital given by the great pianist. The memory of that dazzling occasion never faded. Schumann kept the programme as a 'sacred relic'. Thirty-two years later, when he wrote to Moscheles to thank him for the dedication of the latter's E flat major Cello Sonata, Schumann recalled the event: 'At that time I never dreamed that I should ever be honoured by so celebrated a master.'

Music apart, the other great passion of Schumann's youth was literature. In pursuit of his classical studies he devoured Homer, Cicero, Horace and Sophocles; among German writers, Schiller and Goethe were his idols. At sixteen he helped to run a German Literary Society among Lyceum students, asserting that 'it is the duty of every cultivated man to know the literature of his country'. It sounds like August Schumann talking. He also tried his hand at poetry. Once, he made an abortive attempt to deliver one of his poems 'The Death of

17

Tasso' in public from memory. Halfway through, he forgot it. He was left floundering in embarrassment on the stage. (Thereafter, Schumann retained a lifelong dislike of public speeches; he was often tongue-tied, even in private.) Another great influence was 'Jean Paul', the pen-name of J. P. F. Richter, a German romantic novelist. Jean Paul's highflown literary style made great inroads into Schumann's impressionable mind. This is shown by his juvenile correspondence, which contains some naïve attempts to imitate the master's colourful metaphors.

Nature is the large outspread handkerchief of God, embroidered with His eternal name, on which man can dry all his tears of sorrow, but also his tears of joy, and where every tear drops away into a weeping rapture, and the heart is attuned silently and gently, but piously, to devotion.

(Letter to his mother, 1828)

This is heady prose. Johanna must have gaped in bewilderment. Schumann's touching loyalty to Jean Paul was such that he was apt to regard as a personal enemy anyone whose admiration for him fell short of his own. In 1850, according to Hanslick, the musicians of Hamburg gave a banquet in honour of Schumann. A toast was proposed and Schumann rose to make one of his rare, reluctant speeches. He began by drawing attention to something that everybody in the gathering had overlooked. By a strange coincidence the date was 21 March, the birthday of two of the greatest geniuses of Germany – J. S. Bach and Jean Paul, the immortal rulers of music and poetry. At that point Herr Grädener, director of the Hamburg *Singakademie*, stood up and rather tactlessly declared that Jean Paul could not be mentioned in the same breath as J. S. Bach at a gathering of German musicians. Before Grädener had finished speaking Schumann walked out of the hall in a rage. It took most of the following day before Grädener could calm him down again.

Among August Schumann's business friends in Zwickau was one Carl Erdmann Carus, a wealthy manufacturer and music-lover. His fine home in Zwickau was a rendezvous for local artists. Carus was an enthusiastic amateur violinist, and he arranged frequent performances of classical chamber music for himself and his neighbours. He soon got to hear of Robert's musical gifts, and befriended him. Schumann was everlastingly grateful. When Carus died in 1842 Schumann published an obituary notice in the *Neue Zeitschrift für Musik*.

It was in his house that the names Mozart, Haydn, Beethoven were among those talked of daily with enthusiasm . . . In his house I first got to know the rarer works of these masters.

23 January 1843

An old debt was here repaid.

Carus had a young nephew, Dr. Ernst Carus, who practised medicine at nearby Colditz. He and his wife Agnes were frequent visitors to Zwickau, and took part in these musical evenings. Agnes was a singer of uncommon artistic gifts. She was also good-looking. Robert was captivated by her. He accompanied her in Schubert songs, while silently admiring her. Such was his attachment to Agnes that during the summer holidays he followed her back to Colditz so that they could continue to make music together. This innocent encounter with Agnes was sexually awakening. Robert now graduated to two Zwickau maidens, Nanni Petsch and Liddy Hempel; he enjoyed affairs with them, not one at a time, but simultaneously, a major coup in a small community like Zwickau. He was seventeen.

Among Schumann's youthful compositions are two songs, both dating from his eighteenth year. They are of some interest to us because Schumann later re-composed them and incorporated them into two of his piano sonatas, in which form they are well known. The first one is called 'To Anna'.

[1828]

Here is how Schumann rewrote the song, seven years later, for his Piano Sonata in F sharp minor, op. 11.

[1835]

Aria

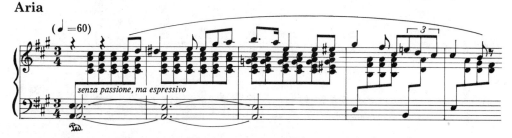

The other song is called 'In Spring'. It gives us a remarkable glimpse of
the mature Schumann, and reminds us that the *Lied* was a form into
which he would later pour some of the world's most significant music.

[1828]

Schumann re-composed that song, as the slow movement of his Piano
Sonata in G minor, op. 22.

[1833–8]

In 1826, Robert's nineteen-year-old sister Emilie killed herself. The unfortunate girl had earlier contracted a skin disease, the psychological effects of which were so unpleasant that they induced a condition of melancholia. Then, during an attack of typhus fever, she left the house and drowned herself. She was a favourite with August Schumann, who never recovered from the blow. A few weeks later, on 10 August, August himself died as well. Johanna Schumann was away at Carlsbad at the time, and the sixteen-year-old Robert had to bear the brunt of the tragedy. The event left a permanent mark on his character. Thereafter, he was totally incapable of facing the thought of death and funerals. (He could not bear to attend his mother's funeral when she died in 1836; yet the journey to Zwickau from Leipzig, where he then lived, took only two or three hours by post-chaise.) August left his family well provided for. Robert inherited 8,000 thalers, a tidy sum then. Today (1973) it would be worth about £12,000. A guardian had been appointed, one Gottlob Rudel, to protect Robert's future and to help administer the boy's share of the estate. Rudel was a cloth and iron merchant who lived in Zwickau. He was once amusingly described to Niecks as 'A stiff business man who looked as if he had swallowed a ruler'.

Johanna, with Rudel's connivance, now insisted that Robert pursue a legal career. She referred to music as 'the breadless art'. August Schumann would have disagreed with her. He had always supported Robert's artistic ambitions. At one point, he had even corresponded with Weber about the possibility of taking Robert as a pupil; unfortunately, nothing had come of the idea. And so, during his final year at the Lyceum, Robert found himself increasingly isolated, being propelled towards a profession for which he had no liking, still less aptitude.

Schumann graduated from the Zwickau Lyceum in March 1828, aged seventeen. He wrote:

School is now behind my back and the world lies ahead. As I went out of school for the last time, I could scarcely suppress my tears; but the joy was still greater than the pain. Now the true inner man must come forward and show who he is.

There were some emotional farewells as Schumann embraced his old friends, the Carus family, Kuntzsch and his mother. Then he boarded the post-chaise and set out for Leipzig.

Schumann Museum at Zwickau

Schumann arrived in Leipzig on 24 March, and at once enrolled as a law-student at the University. He shared rooms with an old Lyceum friend, Flechsig. Since Leipzig's academic term did not begin until May, Schumann now seized the chance to travel. He made friends with Gisbert Rosen, a young law-student who was on the point of migrating to Heidelberg, and together they went off on a tour of Bavaria, visiting Bayreuth, Nuremburg and Munich. The trip was not without incident. At Munich he called on Heine, whose sarcasm and wit made him the talk of Europe. (Heine once wrote of Dreyschock, a rather noisy pianist, that 'one does not seem to hear one pianist Dreyschock, but *drei Schock* [three times three score] pianists'. On another occasion he discovered Meyerbeer's phobia about cats. 'That', Heine remarked, 'is because in a previous incarnation, he was a mouse'!) The great poet received Schumann coolly, little guessing that his own name would soon be linked with that of his young visitor on the highest level of artistic creation. Another treasured encounter was with the widow of Jean Paul in Bayreuth, who gave him a portrait of the master which he packed carefully and sent home to Zwickau.

The most important event of all, however, was his first meeting in Leipzig with Friedrich Wieck and his nine-year-old prodigy daughter Clara. The occasion was a musical party given by Robert's old friends the Carus family, who were now living in Leipzig, and the Wiecks were there as guests. During the course of the evening, Clara played the piano part in a Hummel trio 'amazingly well', according to Robert. The meeting was charged with consequences for all three people; Robert and Wieck exchanged some polite conversation, and arranged a few piano lessons for Robert, laying the foundations of a pupil–teacher relationship which was to last several years. Of Clara herself, Schumann's only comment was that her nose was too long and her eyes too large for her face.

Back from his tour, Schumann attempted to settle down to his law books in Leipzig. He quickly grew bored. The lectures were dull. The university was uninspiring. Above all, he hated law. He called it 'chilly jurisprudence', and said that 'its ice-cold definitions would crush the life out of me'. More than one droning lecturer was abandoned to his fate so that Schumann could return to his rooms to make music. He had acquired a piano. Moreover, among his student friends he had discovered Glock, a cellist, and Täglichsbeck, a violinist. Together they used to play far into the night, Schumann with his shirt-sleeves rolled up, a cigar in his mouth. One of the works chosen for special study was Schubert's Piano Trio in E flat major, a difficult undertaking. Schumann already felt a special affinity with Schubert. He called him 'my only Schubert'. (When Schubert died, later in that same year of 1828, Flechsig reports that he heard Schumann weeping throughout the night.)

Clearly, Schumann's first year at Leipzig was indecisive. To make matters worse, his friend Rosen, now settled in Heidelberg, kept sending back glowing accounts of university life there. Schumann resolved to join him. But what to tell his mother? He soon thought of a suitable excuse. Thibaut, one of the greatest experts on jurisprudence in the whole of Germany, taught law at Heidelberg. He was the author of a *System des Pandektenrechts*, a codification of Roman law as it was practised in Germany, and he was a man of considerable influence in political circles. More important, he was a keen amateur musician, and Schumann knew his book on musical aesthetics, *Purity in Musical Art*. A quick visit was made to Zwickau in order to thrash out the matter with Rudel, his guardian, who agreed to sanction the new arrangement, and Robert set out for Heidelberg in May 1829.

Typically, he combined the journey with a holiday, and made his leisurely way down the Rhine, travelling by post-chaise. Among his travelling-companions was Willibald Alexis, one of the best-selling novelists of his time. (This is hardly surprising when we discover that his early novels were written under the pseudonym 'Sir Walter Scott', an author whom he, to say nothing of the rest of the world, admired.) Alexis took a liking to Robert. The pair did much of their sightseeing together. They visited Goethe's birthplace in Frankfurt, and also called on Ferdinand Ries, Beethoven's former pupil. Robert was captivated by Ries's wife, an English girl 'with the lisp of an angel'. He later remarked that if he ever married it would be to an Englishwoman. His elated mood was reflected in an elaborate practical joke he played while at Frankfurt. Feeling the need to do some piano practice, he walked into a dealer's showroom claiming to be the representative of an English aristocrat who wished to purchase a grand piano. He was shown to an excellent instrument, and practised solidly on it for three hours, finally telling the proprietor that he would return in two days' time with his lordship's decision. 'By that time, however, I was already in Rüdesheim,' wrote Schumann, 'drinking Rüdesheimer.' What the piano dealer said has not been recorded. Schumann finally arrived at Heidelberg on 21 May on foot, and penniless.

Thibaut was more impressive even than Schumann had imagined. He wrote to his mother on 17 July 1829 about the difference between

> . . . the Leipzig professor who stood there like a mechanical toy climbing up the Jacobsladder of automatic promotion, stolidly reading out his lecture notes, as feeble in language as in thought, and Thibaut, who though twice as old is brimming over with life and ideas.

Thibaut became a dominant influence in Schumann's life. Unforgettable hours were spent making music at his house. Every Thursday

24

evening, more than seventy singers were crammed into Thibaut's music-room, with Thibaut at the piano, for a performance of a Handel oratorio. Thibaut lacked any formal training; he held his forces together through personal magnetism. With his flowing, silver-white hair, and his commanding presence, he could produce some riveting effects. Often, he would weep with emotion when the performance had gone particularly well, and silently press Schumann's hand to his own in sheer pleasure. The eighteen-year-old Mendelssohn shared Schumann's enthusiasm for Thibaut, having met him in Heidelberg in 1827. 'It is strange,' said Mendelssohn, 'I understand more about music than he does – yet I have learned ever so much from him, and owe him a very great deal.'

25

The young Schumann, c. 1829

At Heidelberg, Schumann indulged in what can only be described as 'high living'. He developed a taste for cigars and expensive champagne. He did the full round of restaurants and taverns, running up large debts. He attended fashionable balls, carnival masquerades and sleigh-parties. He became a favourite with the local ladies. He boasted in his letters that he was so popular that he was known as 'the darling of Heidelberg'. In money matters, Schumann was irresponsible; at Heidelberg he became a spendthrift, and regularly exhausted his generous allowance. He became, in Niecks's phrase, a master in the art of writing begging letters, a virtuoso in all styles, and poor Rudel, his guardian, must often have been hard put to it to know how to deal with such demands as: 'How much you would oblige me, most honoured Herr Rudel, if you were to send me as soon as possible as much as possible!'

Obviously, there was little time spent on the study of law. To make matters worse, the summer term at Heidelberg was unusually short in 1829. A natural history congress moved into the University; within six weeks, students and professors had dispersed. Schumann saw his chance and was off again, this time to Northern Italy and Switzerland. For the next seven weeks, Johanna and old Rudel were the astonished recipients of a steady stream of letters – a travelogue-by-instalments – as the rake made his leisurely progress through Milan, Brescia and Padua. At Venice he suffered a sharp illness, and loudly complained that he was fleeced by his doctor. Shopkeepers, he swore, always overcharged him because he was a stupid Saxon; so he made himself out to be a Prussian, since Prussians were more highly regarded by the locals, and so successfully did he carry out his masquerade that he was even able to borrow money from a gullible merchant on the strength of it. Italian music did not impress him. He returned to Germany via Switzerland where his amazing obsession with English girls reappeared, and he exchanged 'beautiful glances' with one. His last coup was to raise a loan from an old friend of his father's, Friedrich Kurrer, in Augsburg. He got back to Heidelberg on 20 October, 'as poor as a beggar'.

Somehow he muddled through the winter term, disdaining his law books. His time was devoted almost exclusively to music. It was during this period, in fact, that Schumann composed his *Variations on the name 'Abegg'*, op. 1, for piano. The composition is an important one, for it discloses Schumann's lifelong love of anagrams and puzzles.

Schumann's theme starts by paying this charming tribute to one 'Countess Pauline d'Abegg', to whom the Variations are dedicated.

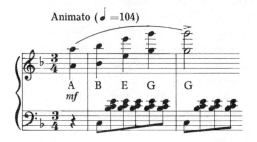

Halfway through, her name is heard backwards.

[N.B. In German B = B♭]

Who was Countess Pauline d'Abegg? Her real name was Meta Abegg, and she was not a countess. Schumann is supposed to have met her at a masked ball in Mannheim during his days as a Heidelberg student. Her pedigree existed only in his colourful imagination. He later described her as 'an old maid of twenty-six, clever and musical, but angular and ugly'. None the less, the theme her name inspired gave Schumann an opportunity for some brilliant variations, which reveal him as a budding virtuoso.

Variation 3

On Easter Sunday 1830, Robert travelled to Frankfurt and heard the great violinist Paganini. The event brought him to the brink of decision. If Johanna had entertained any illusions about Robert as a distinguished lawyer, they were now dispelled. Diplomatically, yet firmly, he prepared her for his true intentions. He wrote to her, euphemistically at first: 'Jurisprudence alone sometimes touches my morning with a nipping little hoar frost.' Then, lest she fail to grasp the point, he added that in Thibaut's view Heaven never meant him for a lawyer. Rudel must have swallowed hard on his ruler. Finally, he tugged at Johanna's heart-strings, reminding her of 'the great spirit of our good father', who had so clearly perceived that his youngest son was destined either for art or for music. His whole case is presented in a letter to his mother dated 30 July 1830. Schumann himself said that it was the most important letter he had ever penned in his life. He got up at 5.00 a.m. to write it.

Heidelberg,
30 July,
5.00 a.m.

Good morning, Mamma!

How shall I describe my bliss at this moment? The spirit-lamp is hissing under the coffee-pot, the sky is indescribably clear and rosy, and the keen spirit of the morning fills me with its presence. Besides, your letter lies before me and reveals a perfect treasury of good feeling, common sense and virtue. My cigar tastes uncommonly good; in short, the world is very lovely at times, if one could only get up early . . . .

My whole life has been a twenty years' struggle between poetry and prose, or, if you like to call it so, Music and Law. . . . At Leipzig I did not trouble my head about my career, but went dreaming and dawdling on and never did any real good. Here I have worked harder, but both there and here have been getting more attached to art. Now I am standing at the crossroads and am scared at the question which way to choose. My genius points towards art, which is, I am inclined to think, the right path. . . .

Now comes the question: 'To be, or not to be', for you can only do *one* thing well in this life, and I am always saying to myself: 'Make up your mind to do one thing thoroughly well, and with patience, and perseverance you are bound to accomplish something.' . . .

28

If I am to go in for music, I must leave at once and go to Leipzig, where Wieck, whom I could thoroughly trust, and who can tell me what I am worth, would then carry on my education. Afterwards I ought to go to Vienna for a year, and if possible study under Moscheles. Now I have a favour to ask you, my dear mother, which I hope you will grant me. *Write yourself to Wieck and ask him point-blank what he thinks of me and my career.* Please let me have a SPEEDY answer, deciding the question, so that I can hurry on my departure from Heidelberg, although I shall be very sorry to leave it and my many kind friends and favourite haunts. *If you like you can enclose this letter to Wieck. In any case the question must be decided before Michaelmas*, and then I shall pursue my object in life, whatever it may be, with fresh vigour and without tears. You must admit that this is the most important letter I have ever written, so I trust you will not hesitate to comply with my request, for there is *no time* to be lost.

Goodbye, dear mother, and do not fret. In this case Heaven will help us only if we help ourselves.

Ever your most loving son,
Robert Schumann

Johanna lost no time in acting on this document. She contacted Wieck at once, asking for his advice and enclosing Robert's letter. Wieck replied immediately and agreed to accept Robert as a pupil, adding: 'I pledge myself to turn your son Robert, by means of his talent and imagination, within three years into one of the greatest pianists now living.' (This was an absurd promise. During the occasional lessons Wieck had given Schumann in 1829, nothing whatsoever had emerged on which he could possibly base such a wild forecast. As we shall see, Wieck had a high opinion of himself, both as a man and as a teacher, and he was prone to boasting.)

And so, after a three-year struggle, Robert finally abandoned law for music; and he did so with Johanna's blessing. He left Heidelberg on 24 September and journeyed to Leipzig to commence his serious music studies under Wieck. A new, and significant, chapter of his life was about to begin. He was twenty years old.

II

The Tyrant Wieck

What kind of man was Wieck? There have been many attempts to sketch his character. He was autocratic, sharp-tongued, categorical, pugnacious even, and he had an obsession for debate which he indulged at the slightest provocation. When crossed, he could fly into a violent temper. He possessed firm convictions about everything, but particularly about piano playing, a topic on which he had lavished much thought, and had now arrived at definite conclusions. He had a reputation for conceit, not entirely undeserved. Once he was talking to Liszt. The conversation switched to music. 'You might have become the finest pianist in the world,' Wieck informed the master calmly, 'if only you had had a proper teacher.'

Wieck was born in Pretzch, a small town on the Elbe, in 1785. He was the second of five sons of an impoverished shopkeeper. His early years were marked by great privation. Thanks largely to the charity of friends, he was able to attend the University of Wittenberg, where he studied theology. Perhaps he was inspired by his grandfather, who was a Lutheran pastor. He was so poor that he might have starved had it not been for the 'charity soup' handed out twice a week. These early struggles left an indelible scar on his personality; they account for his pathological meanness over money matters in later life. In music he was mostly self-taught. 'Helpless and very poor,' he wrote, 'I had to rely solely on my self-education, and on the many chances of my destiny.' By some miracle he managed to acquire a battered old piano, and on this wretched instrument he would practise far into the night. He often fell asleep through sheer exhaustion, elbows on the keyboard, until, waking up again, he would continue with his work. Finding himself unsuited to a theological career (his trial sermon, preached in Dresden, appears to have been a flop), he took a post as a private tutor on the estates of an eccentric nobleman. One of his fellow tutors was Adolf Bargiel, a gifted musician, who later became a well-known piano professor in Berlin and who was eventually to marry Wieck's first wife, Marianne, in 1825. Stimulated by Bargiel's example, and realizing that he would never become a virtuoso, Wieck became fascinated by the theory of piano teaching. He was twenty-eight when he finally set himself up as a piano pedagogue in Leipzig. For the rest of his life the instrument remained his overriding passion. At first pupils were scarce; so Wieck supplemented his income by starting a music lending-library and hiring out pianos. This quickly established connections with touring virtuosi who visited his premises to rehearse their programmes. Within a few years Wieck was acknowledged as the finest teacher in Leipzig.

Wieck's chief qualifications were a keen analytical mind, an unshakeable faith in the rightness of his own views, and a profound conviction that he had a special calling as a teacher. Later events proved him to be absolutely justified. He was an acute observer of pianists and pianos alike. His skill rested on his happy knack of bringing both into a closer and more harmonious relationship. At first he followed Logier's system. Logier had recently invented the 'Chiroplast', a mechanical contraption designed to aid the student towards a correct hand posture, which was then causing great controversy. Subsequently, Logier developed a system of piano teaching, based exclusively on its use, which enabled him to teach a dozen or more students simultaneously. Since they all paid him simultaneously as well, Logier soon became rich. He opened Chiroplast instruction centres all over Europe, laying the foundations of a reputation as a piano teacher which the results hardly justified. Not one pianist of stature was produced by his method. Wieck soon reacted against the 'Chiroplast' which he declared to be a dangerous and damaging contrivance. He went on to develop his own principles of teaching, remarkable for their freedom from pedantry. In a virtuoso age, which insisted on bigger tone and stronger muscles, Wieck stood for a singing touch and a 'quiet' manner at the keyboard. He disapproved of too much practising. He condemned fatigue. He avoided the mindless repetition of isolated passages which lamed talent and killed enthusiasm. He maintained that in order to play the piano at all you must know something about the art of singing – a statement which merits a lot of thought. Unlike his great contemporary Carl Czerny, he refused to teach from morning till

31

night. He deliberately restricted himself to a small handful of carefully chosen pupils, maintaining that each lesson required painstaking preparation – not only from the student, but also from the teacher. His approach to the keyboard is explained in his book *Clavier und Gesang* (1853).

In 1816, when he was past thirty, Wieck married a nineteen-year-old pupil called Marianne Tromlitz. Marianne was a gifted pianist who made several appearances at the Leipzig Gewandhaus concerts in the 1820s. She bore Wieck five children. Since Wieck had resolved that they should all be pianists, their house in the Salzgässchen was filled from morning till night with the strains of practising. On this little world Wieck imposed an iron will. The whole family chafed under his rigorous discipline. After eight miserable years, Marianne could take no more, and she deserted the tyrant taking two of her infants, Clara and Victor, to her parents' home in Plauen. Wieck brought divorce proceedings against her in 1824. As part of the settlement, Wieck was awarded custody of Clara. The child was delivered to him on her fifth birthday. It is indicative of Wieck's unbending character that on the day he divorced Marianne he made the five-year-old Clara start a diary, filling in the first entry himself: 'Today my father divorced my mother.'

From the moment Clara was sent back to her father she fell completely under his domination. Wieck instilled into her the solid virtues of thrift, industry and obedience. She never once questioned her destiny. Even before her birth it had been determined that she should become Wieck's greatest pupil, the finest exponent of his method. Her very name 'Clara' had been chosen to presage her brilliance in the firmament of music.

And now began the years of toil. Father and daughter met daily for lessons. They worked not merely at the piano, but at every branch of music. Clara was taught to revere Bach, Beethoven and Mozart. She was encouraged to compose, and to improvise. Above all, she learned to abhor the shallow and the superficial; it was not for nothing that she was later called the first classical pianist. Wieck brought to music an almost moral outlook. To him, goodness and badness were as real in music as in life. Is it possible that when, years later, Schumann came to write his *Advice to Young Musicians*, and formulated his famous aphorism 'The laws of morality are also the laws of art', he was thinking of Wieck?

Clara Wieck, 1832

Under Wieck's guidance, Clara quickly developed into a magnificent pianist, and she eventually made his name known across Europe. When the tours began, in 1831, Wieck made a great deal of money out of her. Yet he never once exploited the child. Indeed, he had a low opinion of the uncultivated audiences she was sometimes exposed to, 33 and he did his utmost to protect her from their depraved artistic tastes. The stupid concert officials he had to deal with were given short measure. Once, at the equivalent of a 'press conference', Wieck sarcastically noted the 'seventeen questions which were asked him seven hundred times':

Q. When did your daughter begin?
A. Never.
Q. How old is your daughter *really*?
A. That is written under her portrait.
Q. Do not your daughter's fingers hurt her?
A. You forget that you are speaking of Clara Wieck.
And so on, leading to the absurd climax:
Q. Does your daughter like playing?
A. There is an end of everything – even of answers.
Clearly, a difficult man.

Wieck married again in 1828. His choice fell upon Clementine Fechner, the twenty-four-year-old daughter of a clergyman. Despite the difference in age (she was twenty years younger than Wieck) the union was filled with contentment, being terminated only by Wieck's death in 1873, forty-five years later. There were three children of this marriage, and, since Clementine acquired two stepchildren (Clara and Alwin) at the same time as she acquired Wieck, the household now consisted of a large family of seven (see the family tree, p. 120). Wieck moved his brood into a spacious house, No. 36, Grimmaische Gasse, and it was here that he now did all his teaching.

When Robert became his pupil, in October 1830, Wieck was a man of forty-five. As a 'pupil-in-residence' Schumann saw Wieck almost daily. Schumann's immediate intention was to acquire a virtuoso technique. To this end Wieck laid down a rigorous course of study. Clementi's *Gradus ad Parnassum* was almost certainly included; Wieck had often praised these difficult studies which he considered far superior to any by Czerny, who was then more popular. As to the lessons themselves, little is known about the way in which Wieck imparted his knowledge. Certainly, he did very little demonstrating, preferring to sit by his pupils, observing, analysing, explaining. Wieck was not a particularly good pianist; but everyone who heard him play confirmed that he was incapable of producing an unpleasant sound from the piano.

Wieck and Robert were soon at loggerheads. Wieck accused Robert of equating piano playing with 'mechanical dexterity'; accordingly, he concentrated on interpretation. Robert, in turn, accused Wieck of 'rushing' him through the repertoire. (With only three years to 'turn him into one of the greatest pianists now living', time was, admittedly, short.) Matters came to a head in August 1831. Robert wrote to Hummel, told him of his dissatisfaction with Wieck, and inquired about lessons. Then he brazenly informed Wieck of what he had done, explaining, for good measure, that he wished to study with a 'name'. Wieck was thunderstruck. '*Name?*' he shrieked. 'And what of *mine*? Am I not the greatest piano teacher in the world?' He then gave Robert a vigorous tongue-lashing. Robert was not to know it, but he had just enjoyed a dress rehearsal for a whole series of increasingly violent clashes with Wieck in the years ahead.

Schumann stayed no more than a year in Wieck's house. In October 1831 he took up lodgings in the city. Although he continued to see Wieck daily, he now worked as he pleased. His old taste for parties and social life reasserted itself. He surrounded himself with new friends. Schumann's apartments were daily crowded out with young people thinking, talking, arguing about art. Sometimes, they all removed to the local coffee-house (the 'Kaffeebaum', now famous as a result of their visits) and debated far into the night. In later life Schumann referred to them affectionately as 'a group of young hotheads'. Posterity knows them as the starting-point for the 'Band of David'. From this noisy rabble there arose a great idea: the *Neue Zeitschrift für Musik*, through whose pages the 'Band of David' would soon wage war on the 'Philistines' of music. We must shortly consider that battle in more depth (pp. 54ff.).

Robert's theory studies, meanwhile, were supervised by Heinrich Dorn, an eminent academic, who had recently moved to Leipzig from Berlin. The arrangement was sanctioned by Wieck himself. Dorn was a stickler for discipline and excelled in fugue. At first Schumann complained: 'I shall never be able to get on with Dorn: he wishes to get me to believe that music is fugue – Heavens! how different men are.' Later, however, Schumann came to realize the benefits of Dorn's teaching. They kept up a correspondence which lasted until Schumann's death, twenty years later.

In the autumn of 1833, Schumann's circle was enlivened by the appearance of a gifted young newcomer: the pianist Ludwig Schunke. Schunke had been a child prodigy. When he was eleven years old his father had taken him on his first concert tour of Europe. After that, the boy had gone to live with an uncle in Paris, where he studied with Kalkbrenner and Herz. By all accounts, Schunke was a dazzling virtuoso. Thinking that he might make a more successful career for himself in his native land, he returned to Germany and settled in Leipzig. He and Schumann became firm friends. They lodged together in the same house (the corner of Burgstrasse 21 and Sporergässchen). They took up winter-skating together. They haunted the local coffee-houses. Within a few months Schumann was able to say: 'I could do without all other friends for this one alone.' Schunke was possessed of high artistic ideals. He radiated such evangelical fervour that Schumann dubbed him 'the Apostle John'. Once, he got into a heated argument with Nicolai (the composer of *The Merry Wives of Windsor*) and challenged him to a duel. When Schunke discovered that one of Nicolai's seconds was to be Schumann, however, he sued for peace; Schunke and Schumann could never be on opposite sides. Eventually, the friendship was terminated by Schunke's early death from consumption. He was only twenty-three. Schumann was unable to bear the nightly spectacle of Schunke gasping for breath, and he fled temporarily to Zwickau. 'May heaven give me the strength to lose him,' he wrote. Schumann paid an impressive tribute to Schunke's powers as a pianist when he dedicated to him his formidable Toccata, op. 7:

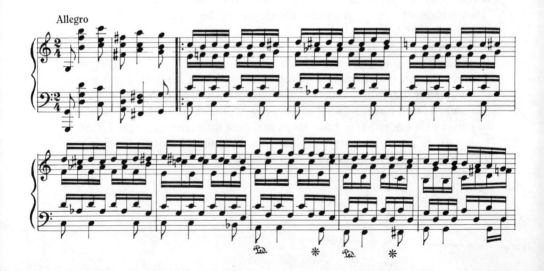

And what of Schumann's own piano playing? In pursuing his technical studies, Schumann had constantly before him the shining example of Clara Wieck, who was now the talk of Leipzig. This eleven-year-old child, with her immaculate technique, must often have given him pause for thought. She was nine years younger than Schumann, but she already had a wonderful command of the keyboard. Schumann must have envied such fluency; Clara accomplished with ease what he himself still had to struggle over. Already, there were signs that Wieck's proud boast to turn Schumann into 'one of the greatest pianists now living' was in serious jeopardy. As early as 1830, and possibly before his lessons with Wieck began, Schumann had made an ominous observation: 'Weakness in my right hand.' A year later, according to Schumann, the hand was now 'lamed'. Then there was that tragic day in 1832 when Wieck returned to Leipzig, after accompanying Clara on one of her sensational tours, only to find Robert with his right hand completely crippled.

III   *A Crippled Virtuoso*

For a hundred years, scholars have wondered about that hand. The traditional explanation of what happened is well known. In a foolhardy attempt to 'equalize' his fingers, Schumann is supposed to have invented a mechanical contrivance – a kind of sling designed to keep one finger out of the way while the others were being exercised – the results of which were disastrous. The tendons of the fourth and fifth fingers of his right hand were supposed to have been permanently injured, bringing his pianistic career to an untimely end. But is the traditional explanation true? Nowhere does Schumann himself specify his injury in this kind of detail. His *Biographische Notizen* (1831) simply contains the laconic entry: 'Overdone technical studies. Laming of my right hand.' Thereafter, Schumann's correspondence refers to his damaged hand only in the vaguest terms. It is as if he himself was at a complete loss to account for the tragedy.

Who started the 'official' story of the finger laming? Wieck did, and we shall shortly understand why. The rumour first appears in Wieck's book, *Clavier und Gesang* (1853). There, Wieck merely says that the 'finger tormentor' was invented 'by a famous pupil of mine, contrary to my wish and used behind my back to the righteous outrage of his third and fourth fingers'. Nowhere does he mention Schumann by name. Later commentators have not been so cautious. Within a few years, this story had crept into the dictionaries and reference books, having collected some interesting variations on the way. Spitta (in *Grove's Dictionary of Music and Musicians*, Vol. I) has Schumann building an 'apparatus', the sinister nature of which is left to his readers' fervid imagination. In a more impressive flight of fancy, Wasielewski has Schumann seeking the assistance of a fellow-student, Töpken, in 'elaborating manipulations'. There are rich possibilities here. The seal of approval was finally given to such rubbish when Eugenie Schumann, the composer's daughter, came forward with her own version of the story. Her father, she announced, had tied up his third finger 'while the others ran up and down the keyboard'. Exactly how he accomplished this miracle remains unclear. In 1889 Frederick Niecks, the Schumann scholar, interviewed Clara Schumann. He

Friedrich Wieck, c. 1870

wanted to clear up the mystery of the crippled hand once and for all. Clara told him quite plainly that the injury was to Schumann's right *index* finger; she added, for good measure, that it was caused through practising on a stiff dumb keyboard. Clearly, her evidence contradicted the accepted story. Niecks disbelieved her. After all, he argued later, she was seventy years old; her memory of those distant events must have failed her. Why Niecks bothered to travel all the way to Frankfurt, simply to accuse Clara of senility the moment she strayed from the conventional line, it is fruitless to conjecture. By rejecting Clara's testimony, Niecks blundered badly. Clara lived on terms of daily intimacy with Schumann for fifteen years. As we shall see, the first part of her observation was absolutely true: Schumann's *right index finger* was the one chiefly affected. As to the cause, it is small wonder that the experts were in disarray. Only in recent years has a convincing medical diagnosis become possible. We are now in a much better position to answer the question: What *was* wrong with Schumann's hand?

In 1971, the English musicologist Eric Sams suggested that Schumann's 'accident' never occurred, at least not in the form generally reported. He offered, instead, the hypothesis that Schumann may have suffered irreversible motor-damage through the absorption of mercury. This is a novel theory, and it deserves the closest scrutiny. The effects of mercury poisoning are well known. Among the first symptoms is paralysis of the extremities, fingers or toes. In order to understand why Schumann was treating himself with mercury, we must understand the disease which killed him twenty-five years later. Schumann himself has left us a great deal of information about the many strange illnesses which plagued him all his adult life (including numbness, slurred speech, convulsions, giddiness, some loss of vision and tinnitus – a ringing in the ears). These symptoms always baffled Schumann's biographers, and they appear to have baffled the medical world as well, to judge by the various diagnoses advanced over the past seventy years – ranging from a brain tumour to schizophrenia. In 1959 two doctors, Eliot Slater and Alfred Meyer, published a joint paper in which they concluded that 'none of these alternatives fits all the facts as well as syphilitic disease'. Now mercury was widely prescribed for syphilis in the nineteenth century. In the developing field of homoeopathy, especially, the substance was regarded as a basic therapy. Among the many doctors Schumann consulted, there were at least two homoeopaths, and a number of quacks. At one point Schumann wrote to his mother: 'My whole house is like a chemist's shop.' In the circumstances, it would have been surprising if Schumann had *not* taken mercury, whose disastrous long-range effects, in other than minute doses, were then little understood. While this explanation must remain circumstantial, it has at least as much to support it (including medical testimony) as the traditional one, which relies largely on hearsay.

There is a remarkable postscript to this story. It shatters the testimony of those 'experts' who, for obvious reasons, identified the wrong finger to suit a favoured theory. It shows that Clara alone told the truth. In 1969 a German scholar was delving into the Leipzig city archives when he came across unpublished correspondence between Schumann and the military commandant there. These letters make it clear that in 1842 Schumann applied for, and was granted, exemption from military conscription on the grounds of his hand injury. He enclosed a medical certificate, signed by his physician Dr. Reuter, which revealed that both the index and the middle finger of the right hand were affected. Schumann would have been unable to work the trigger of a rifle. The world had to wait for 130 years before the final chapter of this fascinating story could be written.

Wieck was appalled by the 'injury'. Perhaps he feared for his reputation as a teacher and wished to guard himself against rumours that he 'forced' his pupils. By publicly condemning the 'finger tormentor' in *Clavier und Gesang* he made his position clear to the entire world. His significant omission of Schumann's name from this context can mean only one thing: Wieck lacked a reason for including it. To accuse Schumann directly of using a 'mechanical aid', he would have been obliged to rig the evidence. As we have seen, Schumann's biographers have not been so hesitant. As for Schumann, the full extent of the tragedy took some time to sink in. A variety of dubious 'cures' were prescribed by his doctors, who urged him to take animal baths (which involved putting his hand into the carcases of freshly slaughtered cattle, a procedure Schumann found distasteful since he feared that something of the nature of cattle might pass into his personality), and to sleep at night with his arm in a herbal bandage. 'The cure is not the most charming,' he wrote, in a masterpiece of understatement. He even travelled to Schneeberg, in 1832, for a course of electrical treatment from one Dr. Otto. It only made matters worse. By the end of 1832 he had lost hope. His short-lived career as a pianist was finished.

In June 1834, a new pupil-in-residence came to live in Wieck's house. She was an attractive eighteen-year-old girl called Ernestine von Fricken. Ernestine, who was born in Asch in Bohemia, was the illegitimate daughter of Baron von Fricken and Countess Zedtwitz. She was a talented pianist, and studied with Wieck until January 1835. Schumann saw her daily, and became infatuated with her; before the year was out the couple were engaged. We shall never know the full story behind their brief entanglement. Within weeks the engagement was broken off by mutual consent. It seems that Ernestine may have been less than frank with Schumann about her illegitimacy, and when he discovered the complications in her family background he was hurt by her silence. Ernestine's later life was clouded by tragedy. She married in 1838. The following year she was widowed. She herself died at the early age of twenty-eight.

Schumann left a characteristic souvenir of his attachment to Ernestine in *Carnaval* (1834–5). About halfway through the piece there is a mysterious movement called 'Sphinxes'. What can it possibly mean?

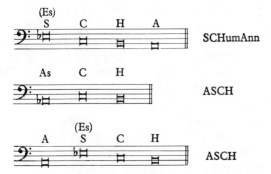

SCHumAnn

ASCH

ASCH   [N.B. In German 'Es' is E flat, 'As' is A flat, and H is B.]

A 'sphinx' was a creature in ancient mythology which posed riddles. Clearly Schumann is setting us a puzzle. If we look at the letters his sphinxes are expressing, however, we discover that he is also presenting us with the solution. 'Asch' was the birthplace of Ernestine. By a strange coincidence, 'Asch' also happens to comprise the only musical letters in Schumann's own name. So Schumann is telling us that he and Ernestine are musically related, and that *Carnaval* is in some way about them both. A glance at the rest of the work soon discloses that the 'Sphinxes' are scattered throughout *Carnaval* and that they generate some of its most important ideas. Here are just seven of them: ⟶

Ernestine von Fricken

a. Reconnaissance

b. Lettres Dansantes

c. Arlequin
Vivo

d. Florestan
Passionato

e. Chiarina
Passionato

f. Estrella
Con affetto

g. Promenade
Con moto

For the rest, notice Schumann's happy choice of archaic notation to symbolize his ancient sphinxes (p. 42). He wished them to slumber silently. Yet how clearly they speak!

Another piece Schumann composed about this time was the *Études Symphoniques*, op. 13. It, too, arose out of Schumann's encounter with Ernestine. Her father, Baron von Fricken, was an amateur flautist. Somehow, Schumann got hold of a theme the Baron had composed and he decided to make it the basis of a large-scale set of piano variations. Each movement is a study in a particular branch of piano technique – chords, pedalling, leaps – and yet at the same time it remains a variation on the Baron's theme:

Andante

The variations themselves reveal Schumann at his most inventive. Here is one ingenious example in which Schumann puts the theme in the bass and unfolds over it a completely new melody with fresh harmonies.

Etude II

Is there a precedent for *Carnaval* and the *Études Symphoniques*? Only by Schumann himself. Here we have a new type of form – a sequence of miniatures, threaded together like pearls on a string, and unfolded in unbroken succession. No one had thought of composing quite like that before. It was Schumann's solution to the problem of large-scale musical structure, a problem which faced all the early Romantics. What shall we call such unusual compositions? The term 'Piano Cycle' seems appropriate. Other famous piano cycles by Schumann are *Kreisleriana*, *Papillons* and *Davidsbündlertänze*.

Perhaps the best known of all the piano cycles is *Kinderscenen* (Scenes from Childhood), a sequence of thirteen pieces, in which Schumann reminisces about childhood. Schumann himself explained that they are an adult's recollection of early youth. One or two reveal a profoundly original view of musical language, and offer a glimpse into Schumann's composing process generally. For example, the fourth piece of the set, called 'Entreating Child', begins with this phrase.

But it also ends with that same phrase.

Schumann has created an idea which is both an antecedent and a consequent. Observe, incidentally, the daring way in which Schumann ends on a dominant seventh chord. The piece 'hangs in space', so to

46

speak, until the next movement enters. This love of 'open-ended' phrases (that is, phrases which can serve both as a beginning and as an ending) remained with Schumann all his life. He used the same technique in 'Prophet Bird' from *Waldscenen* (1849). The phrase

both opens and closes the piece.

    Kinderscenen discloses still another characteristic of Schumann's: his obsession with syncopation. Throughout 'Almost Too Serious', for example, the musical pulse falls in one place and the metre falls in another.

The confusion between ear and eye is all part of its charm. But Schumann sometimes carries this technique to great lengths. In 'Des Abends' (Evening) from *Fantasiestücke*, op. 12, the music sounds as if it is in three-eight time throughout, although it is actually composed in two-eight time.

One piece in *Kinderscenen* which everyone knows is 'Dreaming'. So popular has it become that it has broken away from its companion pieces and assumed an independent existence. Schumann here symbolizes for us all the inner world of the child. $\longrightarrow$

Kinderscenen raises a problem of interest to Schumann's interpreters. One of the oldest stories to attach itself to Schumann is that his metronome was faulty. It is quite untrue, as the English scholar Brian Schlotel has pointed out. For a hundred years or more, however, the experts have told us that his metronome marks are unreliable. Schumann's interpreters, in consequence, have been given a sanction to do whatever they please, a sanction they enjoy with no other major composer. Meanwhile, a performing tradition of Schumann's music has been difficult to establish. It is easy to see how it all came about.

No metronome of Schumann's has survived. We know that he possessed one, however. We also know that it was accurate. This is confirmed in a letter Schumann sent to Ferdinand Böhme, the composer.

Düsseldorf,
8 February 1853.

Dear Sir,
. . . Have you a correct metronone? . . . Mine is accurate. It always gives as many beats to the minute as the number on which the weight is placed. For instance, if the number is 50, it gives 50 beats to the minute; if 60 = 60. And, as far as I know, this is the test of correctness. Perhaps you would try your metronome in this respect.

Clearly, then, Schumann understood the principle on which a metronome functions. His letters contains a strong hint, moreover, that he had checked his own model against a watch – a foolproof test. 'If the number is 50, it gives 50 beats to the minute.' Nor is this all. Schumann maintained a vast correspondence with musicians across Europe about his music. Not once were his tempo indications challenged. He also conducted many rehearsals of his own music, where the players had his printed instructions before them, and nothing emerged to arouse his suspicions. In his own lifetime, in fact, no one ever suggested that his metronome was faulty. So how did the story arise?

Shortly after Schumann's death, in 1856, Clara and Brahms got together to discuss the question of a complete edition of Schumann's

Dreaming

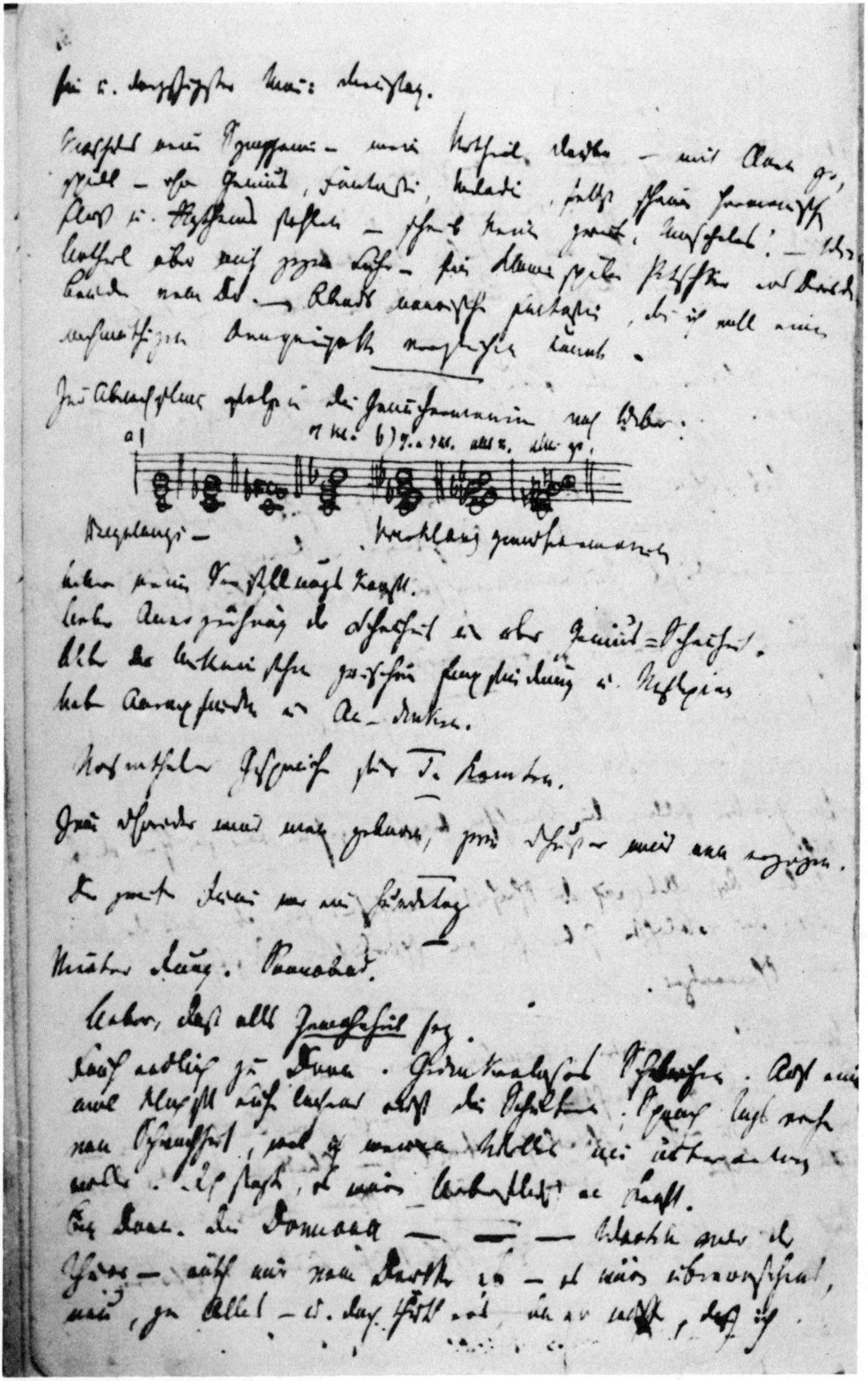

A page from Schumann's diary

music. It was a marathon task, and it occupied them for many years. (The pair eventually produced a twenty-nine volume edition, during the years 1879–93, published by Breitkopf and Härtel.) Clara, of course, had her own ideas about the way in which her late husband's music should be played. She was, after all, one of the great pianists of her time, and a lifelong exponent of Schumann's music. She did not scruple to change Schumann's metronome markings when the spirit moved her, and she doubtless started the rumour that his sometimes 'erratic' tempo markings had a mechanical origin. The proposition seemed reasonable; in the 1840s these rather primitive machines were notoriously unreliable. But it was Hans von Bülow who first made the suggestion in print. He wrote a preface to his edition of the Cramer studies (1869) in which he said: 'It is generally held that Schumann used a defective metronome for an entire creative period.' Fiction soon hardened into fact. Gustav Jansen came forward in 1886, with an edition of Schumann's letters, and announced that Schumann's metronome was not correct, 'as was proved after his death. Consequently, many of his works are wrongly metronomized.' Clara herself set the official seal on this unhappy sequence of events by publishing, in 1887, her 'Instructive Edition' of Schumann's piano music 'based on the manuscripts and the personal tradition of Clara Schumann'.

How much her 'personal tradition' departed from Schumann's can be seen from the following table.

Scenes from Childhood, op. 15

		Robert	Clara
No. 1	Of Foreign Lands and People	♩ = 108	♩ = 108
No. 2	Curious Story	♩ = 112	♩ = 132
No. 3	Catch as Catch Can	♩ = 138	♩ = 120
No. 4	Entreating Child	♪ = 138	♪ = 88
No. 5	Perfect Happiness	♪ = 132	♩ = 72
No. 6	Important Event	♩ = 138	♩ = 120
No. 7	Dreaming	♩ = 100	♩ = 80
No. 8	By the Fireside	♩ = 138	♩ = 108
No. 9	Knight on a Rocking-Horse	♩. = 80	♩. = 76
No. 10	Almost Too Serious	♩ = 69	♪ = 104
No. 11	A Ghost Story	♩ = 96	♩ = 108
No. 12	Child Falling Asleep	♪ = 92	♪ = 80
No. 13	The Poet Speaks	♩ = 112	♩ = 92

We might well ask what kind of metronome Schumann is supposed to have possessed which sometimes ran fast and sometimes ran slow. A faulty metronome, like a faulty watch, can run slow; alternatively, it can run fast. But it cannot run both slow *and* fast.

Once we have accepted the notion that Schumann's tempo markings are there to be followed, the question arises: Why do certain pieces sound uncomfortably fast when played as indicated? All composers know the answer. A mental 'performance' of the score, such as a composer gives himself to check on a new work's progress, can easily sound quicker than it really goes. Set a metronome ticking, and the damage is done. Significantly, none of Schumann's controversial tempi are ever too slow.

Looking back over the period 1830–4, Schumann must have had good cause to feel happy. He had transformed a tragedy into a triumph. The performer in him had been dealt a cruel blow; but the composer in him was now beginning to stir. He had started to revel in his new-found creative powers. Already, aged twenty-five, he had composed a body of piano works destined to take its place among the very greatest master-pieces of music. And Schumann knew that he had yet to give full expression to his genius. There is no happier knowledge for a true creator.

The first issue of the
Neue Zeitschrift für
Musik, *1834*

'Florestan' and 'Eusebius'   IV

Besides Ernestine and *Carnaval*, the year 1834 was notable for yet another event. Schumann had long been dissatisfied with the low standards of music criticism which then prevailed in Germany. As early as 1833 he had discussed with friends and musical acquaintances (usually late at night in the 'Kaffeebaum') the possibility of starting a new magazine which would raise the level of criticism and become a mouthpiece for the rising generation of young Romantic musicians. The *Neue Zeitschrift für Musik* made its bow on 3 April 1834. Many years later Schumann gave his famous account of how the journal was started.

At the end of 1833 a few musicians in Leipzig, mostly young men, found themselves together as though by accident every evening. They met principally to enjoy each other's company; but they were also fully interested in exchanging their ideas about the art that was for them the food and drink of life – music. The state of music in Germany was at that time hardly gratifying. Rossini still ruled the stage; Herz and Hünten, almost by themselves, held the field in piano music. And yet only a few years had passed since Beethoven, C. M. von Weber and Franz Schubert had lived among us. Mendelssohn's star, it is true, was rising, and wonderful things were heard of a Pole, Chopin. But it was only later that they began to exert a lasting effect.

Then, one day, an idea occurred to these young hotheads: 'Let us not look on and do nothing! Take action and improve things! Take action, so that poetic qualities may again be honoured in this art.' In this way originated the first pages of a new musical journal (*Neue Zeitschrift für Musik*).

53

There were only two other magazines of consequence in the whole of Germany. One was called the *Allgemeine musikalische Zeitung*, and its editor was G. W. Fink. Fink was a stuffy conservative; he and Schumann cordially disliked one another. It was only with reluctance that Fink, two years earlier, had been persuaded to publish the twenty-one-year old Schumann's now famous review of Chopin's 'Là ci darem' Variations, with its resounding imperative: 'Hats off, gentlemen, a genius!' (Schumann never forgave Fink for printing only the first half of that review. The second half is lost.) The other magazine was called *Iris im Gebiert der Tonkunst*, and its editor was Ludwig Rellstab. He was notorious for the malice in his reviews. His criticism of the soprano Henrietta Sontag, in which he satirized a respected diplomat, earned him a three-month stretch in Spandau prison. (Rellstab is probably the only critic in history to go to jail for his views.) It served merely to enhance his reputation. Shortly afterwards, he was appointed to the Berlin newspaper *Vossische Zeitung*, and from this elevated position he dealt out even more death and destruction. Fink and Rellstab, then, were diametrically opposed. Schumann had no time for either of them; he was convinced he could beat them both at their own game. The *Neue Zeitschrift* was to prove him right.

At first, Schumann was assisted in the project by Wieck, Schunke and Julius Knorr (who was nominated its first editor-in-chief). Within a few months, however, Schunke was dead, Knorr was ill, and Wieck had lost interest. Schumann was left to take over the entire project himself. Under his guidance, the *Zeitschrift* trounced its rivals and became the most influential journal of its time, with a wide circulation throughout Germany. Such was its success that for many years Schumann was far better known to the outside world as a critic than as a composer.

What was the *Zeitschrift* about? Certainly, there has never been another journal to compare with it. A glance through its pages discloses a whole new philosophy of musical criticism. The first thing to strike one is the style of writing – lively, witty, exuberant, fanciful, some of it even in dialogue – quite unlike the stiff and stodgy prose which then did duty for musical criticism. Much more tantalizing was the appearance of a colourful group of writer-musicians calling themselves the *Davidsbund* – the 'Band of David' – who seemed to turn up in every issue, argue among themselves, make outrageous statements, and dominate the list of contributors. The *Davidsbund*, in fact, was a fictitious society of musicians, created within Schumann's imagination, for the express purpose of fighting the Philistines in music.

Well might the first readers of the *Zeitschrift* ask, bewildered, who the members of the 'Band of David' were. Even today, the identity of some of them is blurred. One or two names stand for Schumann himself; others were invented for friends and colleagues. The choice of pseudonym depended entirely on the tone of Schumann's review. Thus, 'Florestan' and 'Eusebius' represent the twin sides of Schumann's own personality – the passionate man of action and the gentle dreamer respectively. 'Master Raro', on the other hand, is the all-round musician, renowned for the sanity of his judgements; several biographers think he stands for Friedrich Wieck, but this is unlikely in view of the fact that Schumann and Wieck rarely saw eye to eye on musical matters. Riemann made the interesting discovery that if you place Clara's name with Robert's, end to end, you get 'claRARObert', which suggests an altogether different derivation. Schumann's rival for Clara's affections, Karl Banck, is appropriately called 'Serpentinus', and one wonders whether he knew about, let alone approved of, a nickname which depicts him crawling on his belly. Schumann made great sport with his rival editor Fink, whom he caricatured with the reversed form of his name, 'KNIF'. It provoked a rage in Fink who came out with a (for him) steaming article. '*Bündler* to the right of us, *Bündler* to the left of us, Figaro here, Figaro there,' and he went on defiantly: 'but to date, we are still here at the old stand.' Alas, Fink was whistling in the dark. His days were numbered. He went into retirement in 1841. His editorial desk was taken over by C. F. Becker, a friend of Schumann's, and a regular contributor to the *Zeitschrift*.

The *Davidsbund* took such a hold on Schumann's imagination that he even signed some of his latest compositions with their names. His Piano Sonata in F sharp minor, op. 11, for instance, originally bore the inscription:

Piano Sonata
Dedicated to Clara
by Florestan and Eusebius
op. 11

Nowhere does Schumann's own name appear. Again, the public might ask, who were 'Florestan' and 'Eusebius'? Why the pseudonyms? To intrigue people, to take them by storm. And in those days, the idea of leaving off the dedicatee's last name was unheard of.

Sometimes, the *Davidsbund* actually turn up in Schumann's music. Both 'Florestan' and 'Eusebius' are immortalized in the great piano cycle *Davidsbündlertänze*. This is a sequence of eighteen pieces, each one of which is signed 'E' or 'F', or sometimes 'E and F', depending on the mood of the music. Occasionally, programmatic allusions adorn the score. 'Here Florestan kept silent, but his lips were quivering with emotion.' And Schumann quotes an old German proverb on the title-page:

> Along the way we go
> Are mingled weal and woe,
> In weal, though glad, be grave,
> In woe, though sad, be brave

which sets the scene for the dialogue running through the music. Here is one of Schumann's tranquil depictions of 'Eusebius', the introspective dreamer.

We also find musical portraits of 'Florestan' and 'Eusebius' in *Carnaval*. The stormy passions which overcome 'Florestan' boil over in the sixth number of the cycle:

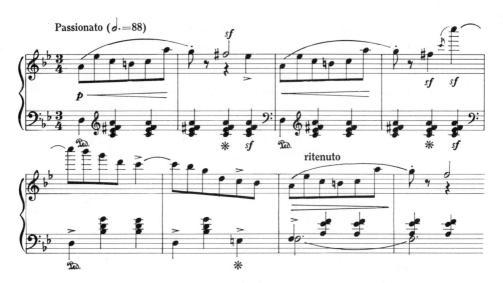

At the conclusion of *Carnaval*, in fact, the struggle between the 'Band of David' and the 'Philistines' is symbolized by the *Marche des Davids-bündler* in which the Philistines are caricatured with a quotation from the then popular 'Grandfather's Dance' – a seventeenth-century tune which not only puts them to flight but which, because of its connotation, puts them to shame as well.

Schumann's highly individual philosophy of music may seem puzzling at first. Where did he get all these colourful ideas? From Jean Paul, whose novels exemplified the Romantic literary theory of double personality. Schumann knew every page of *Die Flegeljahre*, whose characters 'Walt' and 'Vult' depict the contrasting halves of Jean

57

Paul's own character. (The best-known novel in English to illustrate this theory is *The Strange Case of Dr. Jekyll and Mr. Hyde*.) The introspective, inward-looking half of human nature is (according to the theory) balanced by the extrovert, outward-looking half – and it was this idea which led to the creation of 'Florestan' and 'Eusebius', the twin halves of Schumann's own musical personality. This is what Schumann meant when he once said that he had learned more counterpoint from Jean Paul than from any of his music teachers. Certain commentators, looking for trouble, have seen 'Florestan' and 'Eusebius' as early symptoms of a split in Schumann's mind. There is, however, nothing sinister about Schumann's literary creations; and there is nothing difficult about the Romantic theory of literature which gave them birth. The nineteenth century had just seen the emergence of a new and exciting discipline – psychology. No longer was it possible for novelists to present their characters in simple, black and white terms. Human nature was seen to be too deep for that. Heroes could also be villains; saints could also be sinners. And critics? A critic could be a sage and a simpleton. How much truer to let out both sides of his character simultaneously! In creating his 'Band of David', then, Schumann was behaving like a true child of his age. As Schumann himself put it, with perfect clarity, just two years before his death: '*In order to express contrasting points of view about art*, it seemed not unfitting to invent antithetical artistic characters of which "Florestan" and "Eusebius" were the most important, with "Master Raro" as intermediary.'

The Struggle for Clara   V

When Schumann took up residence at Wieck's house, in 1830, he was
twenty years old. Clara was eleven. Despite the nine-year difference in
their ages, there sprang up between them a bond of mutual affection.
This was hardly surprising: Schumann, who was treated like one of the
family, saw Clara almost daily. At first, Robert assumed the role of an
elder brother; there were long rambles together in the countryside,
hilarious games of blind-man's-buff with her young brother Alwin, and
ghost stories told by Schumann with such relish (he was a wonderful
mimic) that the children shrieked with fright. Soon there were signs of
deeper feelings stirring within them. Then came Ernestine von Fricken.
Clara could not compete with the older girl either physically or intel-
lectually. Throughout the summer and autumn of 1834, while
Schumann's affair with Ernestine progressed towards its unhappy
close, Clara (as she later confessed in her letters) felt cut off from
Robert's affections. It came as a relief to her when Ernestine retired
from the scene for good. By November 1835 Clara and Robert had
declared their love for one another.

  Wieck was not blind to what was going on. Clara was developing into
a striking young woman, mature above her years. Robert was now her
constant companion. Infatuation was one thing; a love-affair was quite
another. Wieck thought it wise to take defensive measures. In January
1836 he removed Clara from Leipzig to Dresden, thinking to break her
association with Robert. This was an extreme step, and Wieck doubtless
congratulated himself on its effectiveness. But he reckoned without
Schumann. While Wieck was unexpectedly called away from Leipzig
on business, Robert seized the opportunity to travel to Dresden (about
fifty miles away) and visit Clara. On his return, Wieck was informed of
the fact, and broke into a torrent of abuse against the luckless pair.   59

He thoroughly frightened Clara by threatening to shoot Schumann if he ventured near the girl again. Then he forbade Schumann to enter his household. Clara was brought back to Leipzig, under strict surveillance. Her mail was opened; she was not allowed out alone; even her bedroom door had to remain unlocked. Small wonder that Schumann, faced with such stringent behaviour, nicknamed Wieck *Rappelkopf* – 'crackpot'.

If we wish to understand Wieck's attitude towards Robert, we must first understand his attitude towards Clara. Clara was more than a daughter: she was Wieck's special creation, his life's work. For years, he had coached her at the piano. She was now his star pupil, the finest exponent of his method. She was also a valuable commodity, much sought after. She boosted Wieck's bank balance at the same time as she boosted his ego, and Wieck found the combination highly agreeable to him. Wieck, in short, was professionally involved. His uncompromising character did the rest.

Robert had no notion of the protracted struggle which lay ahead of him. For one thing, he was constitutionally incapable of understanding Wieck's complex make-up. For another, he made the elementary blunder of supposing that it was he, Schumann, to whom Wieck was personally opposed. Nothing could be further from the truth. Wieck would have opposed anyone who threatened his special relationship with Clara. And he would have fought back with exactly the same weapons – invective, deceit, libel, even violence – which he eventually brought to bear against Schumann.

The first hint of the granite-like character Schumann was up against came in September 1837. Schumann gambled everything on a letter to Wieck in which he declared his love for Clara, and requested an interview: 'You owe it to my position, my talent and my character.' The letter was tactfully delivered to the old man on 13 September, Clara's eighteenth birthday. A few days later, Robert was ushered into the presence. He had not set foot in the Wieck household for over a year. There was a scene. Wieck was quite implacable. Robert later wrote to Clara: 'My interview with your father was terrible. He was frigid, hostile, confused and contradictory at once. Truly his method of stabbing is original, for he drives in the hilt as well as the blade.' Wieck's chief objection was that Clara was to be a concert pianist, not a *Hausfrau*. He poured scorn on the idea of 'Clara with the perambulator'. And so began the long and sordid quarrel between Wieck and Schumann which lasted for three years and culminated in a lawsuit.

Autograph page of Piano Sonata in F minor, Op. 14

In desperation, Schumann now thought of moving the *Zeitschrift* to Vienna. Was not Vienna the musical capital of the world? Beethoven and Schubert had lived and worked there. Surely, he argued, once he and Clara were established in this artistic haven, all Wieck's attempts to meddle in their private lives would be frustrated. So, in the autumn of 1838, Schumann set out for Vienna, bubbling over with enthusiasm at these wonderful prospects. He was doomed to disappointment. The local publishers were hostile. The last thing they wanted was competition from the highly successful *Zeitschrift*. Also, Schumann discovered that the Vienna press was stifled by censorship; the city was then in political turmoil. Whatever else happened, Schumann was determined

61

that the *Zeitschrift* should not be muzzled. Sadly, he decided to return to Leipzig.

It was while he was visiting the Austrian capital, however, that an event occurred which redeemed all his disappointments. It reads like fiction. Schumann assures us it was fact.

Like many musicians before and since, Schumann took the opportunity to visit the tombs of Beethoven and Schubert. In those days they slumbered three graves apart in the Währing Cemetery. He was looking at Beethoven's grave, paying his respects, when he observed a steel pen lying on the headstone. The pen was in perfect condition, and Schumann pocketed it as a souvenir. He took it to be a good omen. (In a way, it was; he later composed his 'Spring' Symphony with this pen.) On the way back from the cemetery, the thought occurred to him that Schubert's brother Ferdinand still lived in the city, and he experienced an irresistible desire to look him up. The visit turned out to be historic. During the conversation, Schumann discovered that Ferdinand still had in his possession a number of Schubert's manuscripts. With unerring critical insight, the young man quickly selected from this priceless collection the undisputed masterpiece – the 'Great' C major Symphony. He immediately sent the score to Mendelssohn who gave the first performance of the 'Great' C major at a Gewandhaus concert in Leipzig on 21 March 1839. It was an instantaneous success. Mendelssohn promised the Leipzigers he would repeat it the following year. On the night of 12 March 1840, the Gewandhaus was packed out. The Symphony began. The orchestra had just reached the second subject:

when firebells were heard clanging past the hall. The building now emptied somewhat quicker than it had filled. Fortunately, the Gewandhaus itself was not in danger, but the performance was ruined. In order not to disappoint the audience, Mendelssohn scheduled two further performances later that year which took place without incident. Schumann himself fills in the background to these unusual events, including finding his lucky pen, in an article in the *Zeitschrift* published in 1840.

The years 1835–40, then, were turbulent ones. And the struggle for Clara was draining Schumann dry. When we look at his music, it is hardly surprising that Clara, who obsessed him in life, also obsessed him in art. The most significant composition of this period is the *Fantasie* in C major, op. 17 (1836). Conceived on the grandest scale, the work takes about half an hour to perform. Schumann told Clara: 'It is a profound lament about you.' This was not idle sentiment. The *Fantasie* symbolizes Clara in the most concrete terms, as we shall presently discover.   ⟶

The *Fantasie* is really a vast, three-movement sonata, and 'Grand Sonata' was what Schumann first called it. The historical background to the work is relevant. In the 1830s a Beethoven Memorial Committee was set up to raise funds for the erection of a statue to the master. Musicians across Europe were invited to contribute. Schumann thought that the best way he himself could participate would be to compose a work in memory of Beethoven, whom he revered, and offer the royalties to the Committee. Accordingly, he embarked on a composition which, he said, was meant to depict the life of Beethoven. Programmatic titles adorned the movements – 'Ruins', 'Triumphal Arch', 'Wreath of Stars' – like some tribute to a Greek hero. Later, this idea was dropped, and the work was eventually published as a *Fantasie*, with a dedication to Liszt (who had nobly offered to bear the brunt of the cost of the monument). At the head of the score stands this motto by Schlegel:

> Through all the tones
> In Earth's many-coloured dream
> There sounds one soft-drawn note
> For the secret listener.

Who is 'the secret listener'? What is the 'long-drawn note'? Schumann scholars have pondered these questions for a hundred years. Schumann himself gives us a clue. He wrote to Clara: 'Tell me what occurs to you when you hear the first movement of the Fantasie? . . . Are you not the "note" in the motto? I almost believe you are.'

So Clara herself is 'the note in the motto'. Therefore she ought to be symbolized in the music. And so she is – for the secret listener. Remember the historical background to the work. The music is about Beethoven as well as Clara. Schumann, therefore, uses a symbol which reminds him of them both. He weaves into the music a quotation from

63

Fantasie in C major

Beethoven's song cycle *An die ferne Geliebte* (To the Distant Beloved):

Beethoven's original runs:

The words say: 'Accept, then, these melodies that I sang for you, my love.' They make it plain that the 'distant beloved' was Clara. Incidentally, does not the 'distant beloved' already shimmer behind the first page of the music? But perhaps you have to be a 'secret listener' to hear it.

The second movement is a March, and it contains some of the most difficult keyboard music Schumann ever composed. Its main theme unfolds like this:

Clara was bowled over. 'I have already learnt the March from the *Fantasie*, and revel in it!' she wrote. 'It makes me hot and cold all over.' Her symptoms are shared by pianists even today.

Everyone thinks of late Beethoven when they hear the finale – a slow movement of great spirituality. Perhaps Schumann intended them to, since this was the movement he originally called 'Wreath of Stars' when it was first conceived as a tribute to his musical hero.

The *Fantasie* raises the neglected question of Schumann's deep affinity with Beethoven. His 'Beethoven quotations' could fill a volume. Sometimes the allusions are made tongue-in-cheek. There is, for instance, an amusing connection between his 'Soldier's March' (from *Album for the Young*):

and the Scherzo from Beethoven's 'Spring' Sonata, op. 24:

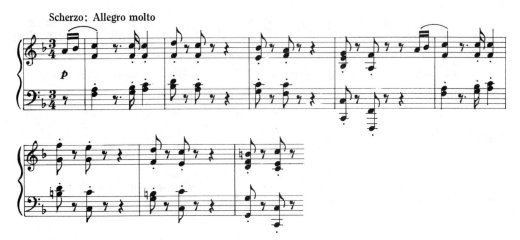

The one sounds like a parody of the other. Consider also the following passage from the 'Presto Passionato', the alternative finale Schumann wrote for his well-known Sonata in G minor, op. 22:

This is a clear allusion to Beethoven's 'Kreutzer' Sonata, op. 47:

And perhaps the most obvious quotation of all occurs in the finale of *Carnaval* (the 'March of the Davidsbündler'):

67

Molto più vivace

where we get a definite glimpse of Beethoven's 'Emperor' Concerto:

Allegro

It was now 1839, and Schumann's lawsuit against Wieck was coming to the boil. Wieck's 'defence' rested on the flimsiest grounds. He maintained that Schumann could not afford to marry, and he complained of his 'drinking habits'. Schumann had little difficulty in disposing of both charges. He produced figures to show that his annual income was well above average (the *Zeitschrift* made a handsome profit for him), and he found witnesses to testify to his sobriety, including Mendelssohn, Ferdinand David and Count Reuss. It was far more difficult to deal with the slanderous gossip Wieck spread through his network of friends and associates in and around Leipzig; this was calculated to do Schumann the maximum harm and to discredit him in the eyes of the world. Wieck did not hesitate to dredge up the Ernestine Fricken affair, and he tried, in vain, to enlist her help in blackening Schumann's character. He even stooped to encouraging one Karl Banck, a friend of the family, and Clara's singing-teacher, to flirt with Clara, rightly calculating that when Schumann heard about it he would be upset. Since the two lovers had no way of meeting, it was impossible for either one of them to reveal Wieck's mendacity to the other. For much of the time Clara was on tour with Wieck; her only means of communication with Schumann was a clandestine correspondence which was in constant danger of interception by Wieck himself. It soon became apparent to Schumann that in view of Wieck's implacable attitude they would have to go over his head and apply to the law courts for permission to marry. Clara found herself torn between her lover and her father, whom she still deeply respected. It was not until September 1839 that Schumann finally persuaded her to sign the affidavit. She later wrote: 'The instant when I signed was the most important of my whole life. I set my name down with firm resolution, and was boundlessly happy.'

Wieck's reaction was one of frenzied rage; he refused to have her in the house and she went to live temporarily in Berlin with her mother. By his extreme behaviour, Wieck turned himself into a laughing-stock. He wrote to dealers advising them not to let Clara play their pianos, else the action might be damaged. He tried to drive away her audiences; he spread reports of her 'shameless' behaviour and described her as 'a miserable, demoralized girl'. And all this from a man who, as Schauffler points out, once wrote in Clara's diary this pious utterance: 'Let your highest goal be the forming of your charge into a good person!' Whenever he met Schumann in the street, he spat in his face. He finally drew up an impossible document setting out the basic conditions under which he would consent to the marriage. The couple were not to live near Wieck; Clara must give up her savings; and so on.

The terms were totally unrealistic. In an attempt at conciliation, the couple sent Einert, a Leipzig lawyer, to present their case in person. The uncontrollable Wieck screamed that he would enforce his will, 'though it meant the destruction of thirty people' – a remark worthy of Caligula. 'What a man!' was Schumann's comment. There was a second attempt at conciliation in December 1839. The parties met in court, and Wieck became so abusive he had to be silenced by the judge. He appears to have had no legal representation, and was thus a perfect example of the old adage that a client who conducts his own defence has a fool for a lawyer. The judge evidently agreed; he threw out Wieck's case, but gave leave of appeal. Wieck used the respite for a reckless counter-attack. In January 1840, when it looked as if he was about to lose the legal fight for Clara, he forged a letter containing all kinds of accusations against Schumann, which he signed 'Lehmann'. Wieck then arranged for this squalid document to be delivered to Clara on the day of her great Berlin recital, hoping so to undermine her confidence that the result would be an artistic disaster. Fortunately, Clara's young brother Alwin discovered the plot and alerted Schumann who, in turn, warned Clara of the letter's impending arrival. Schumann now charged Wieck with slander, and brought a separate libel action against him. (It

69

dragged on until 1841, when it was finally settled in Schumann's favour.)
Wieck now found himself fighting on two fronts simultaneously.
Moreover, he knew he was already discredited in Clara's eyes. A pyrrhic
victory was not to his taste. The fight went out of him. Weeks, then
months, ticked by. The courts waited until August when, having
received no further word from Wieck, they gave judgement in favour of
Robert and Clara. The wedding banns were published on 16 August,
and the wedding ceremony itself took place on Sunday 12 September in
the village of Schönfeld. Robert may well have chosen the day in order
to spite Wieck. The reason is obvious. The next day was Clara's twenty-
first birthday. 12 September, then, was the last day on which Wieck
could be legally defied – a parting shot from Robert.

Robert's marriage to Clara was heralded by an event of major creative
significance. It never ceases to astonish us. To find a parallel we must go
back to Schubert and Mozart. Between March and July 1840, in an
inspired stream of creative effort, Schumann composed five of history's
greatest song cycles: *Liederkreis*, opp. 24 and 39, *Dichterliebe*, *Myrthen*,
and *Frauenliebe und -leben*. He was in his thirtieth year. Clara was his
inspiration. Has any woman received such a wedding gift as the
manuscript of 'Mondnacht' (from *Liederkreis*, op. 39)?

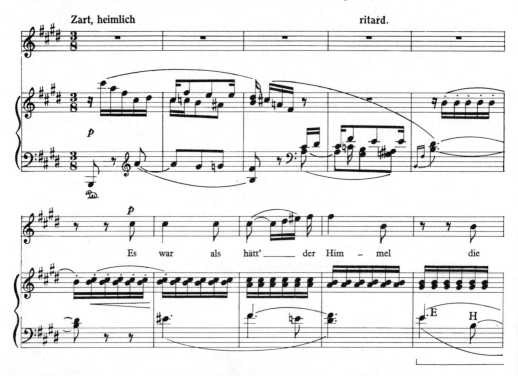

The notes 'EHE' mean 'marriage' in German. They are woven into the very fabric of the song. Given the biographical background, can we doubt that Schumann was once again addressing Clara in the most direct possible manner?

Schumann scholars still refer to 1840 as the 'song year', when more than 140 songs flowed from his pen. There were periods when Schumann averaged several songs a day. On 21 February, for instance, he put down twenty-seven pages of *Myrthen* in a state of creative elation 'about which I can say nothing more than that I laughed and cried for joy.' The astonishing thing is that he came so late to the art of song. Even as recently as 1839 he wrote that he 'considered vocal composition inferior to instrumental music – I have never regarded it as great art.' The conversion, when it came, was spectacular. His new passion took such a compulsive hold on him that he tried to fight it. 'But I cannot do anything else – I must sing myself to death like a nightingale.'

If Schumann had composed nothing but songs, he would still be a major master. His profound literary taste instinctively led him to the greatest poets – Heine, Goethe, Eichendorff and Rückert among them. Among his innovations was to scatter thematic relationships throughout the various songs of a cycle. Another was to liberate the piano, hitherto a subservient accompanist. In Schumann the piano not only becomes an equal partner, but it occasionally dominates the composition. For instance, *Dichterliebe* closes with an epilogue for solo piano in which the singer stands on the platform, a hushed spectator to the inspired stream of music the keyboard now pours forth. Here, music literally begins where words leave off: $\longrightarrow$

In the popular imagination, Robert and Clara are frequently depicted as an ideal couple, each one serving as a perfect complement to the other. Yet it is not true that theirs was a relationship without stress. There was not only the inevitable tension between them, caused by the ordinary pressures of domestic routine; frequently, there was a serious clash of artistic interests as well, which caused damaged feelings on both sides. Clara's piano-playing was the first casualty. After only five months of marriage, we find her complaining to her diary: 'My playing is getting all behindhand, as is always the case when Robert is composing. I cannot find one little hour in the day to myself! If only I did not get so behind!' Schumann was well aware of the difficulty, and felt guilty about it. 'I am often sorry that I so frequently hinder Clara in her study, because she will not disturb me when I am composing.' Worse was to follow, however. In 1842, the couple went on tour. At Oldenburg an invitation to visit the Court arrived for Clara alone. Robert felt the insult deeply; the implication was obvious: Clara was well known but who was her husband? The incident so marred the tour that Schumann returned to Leipzig while Clara went on to Copenhagen

by herself. Again, during the Russian tour of 1844, Robert's subordinate position was continually painful to him. While Clara was enjoying a huge popular success at her concerts, Robert, trailing behind, was introduced to everybody as 'the pianist's husband'. It is to the ever-lasting credit of both of them that they were able to rise above such

73

stresses. Schumann himself saw their peculiar situation with absolute clarity, and expressed it thus:

> Well, so must it be when artists marry; one cannot have everything; and after all the chief thing is the happiness which remains over and above, and we are happy indeed in that we possess one another and understand one another, understand and love with all our hearts.

Autograph page of Humoreske, *Op. 20*

Leipzig

Leipzig, where the Schumanns now settled, was fast becoming one of the important musical centres of Germany. Forty thousand people dwelt there. The great printing house of Breitkopf and Härtel had its home there. A hundred years earlier Bach had lived and worked there. The church of St. Thomas still housed many of his forgotten manuscripts. Soon the 'Bach revival' would get under way and make Leipzig world-famous. The Gewandhaus concerts, subsidized by the linen-merchants of Leipzig and held in their ancient market-hall, had a distinguished history stretching back to the first half of the eighteenth century; they were now approaching their most glorious epoch. Already there was talk of founding a Conservatory of Music. Within three years, in fact, a group of wealthy businessmen had put up the required capital and launched an institution which was to attract some of the most brilliant names in music. Leipzig was a practical place for musicians to be in 1840. Robert and Clara lived there for four years.

At the heart of Leipzig's musical life stood Felix Mendelssohn. This young genius towered over his contemporaries. When he was only twenty-six years old, and already a composer of European fame, he had been appointed conductor of the Gewandhaus concerts. Under his inspired leadership, the Gewandhaus became a kind of musical shrine at which the faithful gathered regularly to hear the masterpieces of Beethoven, Schubert and Bach brought to life by this incomparable musician. Schumann stood in awe of him and of his unique gifts; he called Mendelssohn 'the Mozart of the nineteenth century'. In 1843 Mendelssohn founded the Leipzig Conservatory of Music and appointed to its teaching staff such names as Moscheles (piano), David (violin), Hauptmann (theory) and Schumann himself for composition and piano. Through sheer force of artistic personality, Mendelssohn welded together this loose band of musicians and gave them a higher artistic purpose. Within ten years, he had led Leipzig out of its quiet cultural backwater into the mainstream of Europe's musical life.

Another of Schumann's friends was the English composer Sterndale Bennett. Bennett had been an infant prodigy, entering the Royal Academy of Music before his tenth birthday. When he was only seventeen he was spotted by Mendelssohn who was on a visit to London and heard the youth play his own Piano Concerto in D minor in the Hanover Square Rooms. Mendelssohn was impressed. He immediately invited Bennett to Leipzig. 'If I come, may I be your pupil?' 'No, you must come as my friend.' Bennett made his Leipzig début at a Gewandhaus concert in 1837. Sitting in the audience was Schumann who covered the event for the *Neue Zeitschrift*. 'We cannot but marvel at this early-developed master-hand. . . . Here we have to do with an artist of the higher orders.' Naturally, the two musicians became friends, and Bennett was soon introduced to Clara. Here he may have blotted his copy-book. She played him her Piano Concerto. Asked his opinion, he replied: 'It requires weeding.'

Niels Gade was also a member of the Leipzig circle. He achieved fame overnight by winning first prize in a Copenhagen competition with his overture *Echoes of Ossian*. In 1843 he settled in Leipzig, and Mendelssohn appointed him deputy conductor of the Gewandhaus concerts. He became friendly with Schumann who supported him enthusiastically in the *Neue Zeitschrift*. Schumann soon observed that the letters in Gade's name are all to be found in the musical alphabet. With his special flair for puzzles and anagrams he at once devised the following:

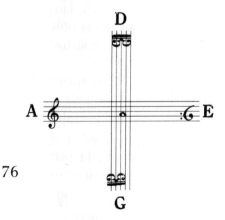

Read it clockwise, starting with the tenor clef.

One of the *Album for the Young* pieces (called 'Northern Song') contains Gade's name. It begins: ⟶

Schumann's relationship with Liszt was more complex. It started out enthusiastically; later it was marred by a foolish quarrel over Mendelssohn. Schumann first met Liszt in 1840, when Liszt, in the middle of those historic European tours of his which brought him both fame and notoriety, stopped at Leipzig to give concerts. After their first meeting Schumann declared: 'It is as if we had known one another for twenty years.' Eventually, however, Schumann reacted against Liszt's flamboyant personality. He came to accept Mendelssohn's description of him as 'a continual alternation between scandal and apotheosis'. Clara did not help matters. She called Liszt 'a smasher of pianos'. As Schumann's own involvement with piano virtuosity waned, he, too, came to despise Liszt's spectacular brand of keyboard fireworks. By 1850 the two musicians were hardly on speaking terms.

Im Volkston   **Northern Song**

In order to understand what happened, we have to go back a bit. In June 1848 Liszt paid the Schumanns a surprise visit at Dresden. Clara went to considerable pains to arrange a musical dinner in his honour. A time was fixed, and musicians were assembled. Unfortunately, Liszt was delayed. The exasperated players, having started a performance of Beethoven's D major Trio in their guest of honour's absence, were rudely interrupted as Liszt walked in, two hours late. Schumann's Piano Quintet followed, which Liszt tactlessly described as 'Leipziger-isch'. There was tension in the air throughout dinner. Then an argument broke out about the respective merits of Mendelssohn and Meyerbeer. Liszt praised Meyerbeer at Mendelssohn's expense. At this, Schumann exploded. He seized Liszt by both shoulders and shouted in a rage: 'Who are you that you dare to speak in such a way of a musician like Mendelssohn?' He then rushed out of the room and slammed the door, leaving the others glaring at Liszt in silence. Liszt rose to the occasion superbly. He turned to Clara and said: 'Madam, please tell your husband that he is the only man in the world from whom I would take so calmly the words just offered to me.' The story is told by Gustav Jansen. Schumann's outburst can only be understood in the light of Mendelssohn's death which had occurred just a few months earlier.

As we shall see, there was a good deal of background to this 'scene'. It neatly symbolized the historic split between the Leipzig and Weimar schools. Liszt's continual references to 'Leipziger-isch' were aimed at that band of musicians centred around the Leipzig Conservatory – among them Schumann's colleagues Rietz, Hauptmann and David. He regarded them as narrow academics, and nicknamed them 'little Leipzigers'. The very year of his quarrel with Schumann (1848), Liszt had settled in Weimar and was now busily turning it into a centre for modern music. Leipzig and Weimar were soon fierce rivals and the struggle between them was to dominate the historical scene for about twenty years. Broadly speaking, Liszt reacted against Classical models. He abandoned the 'abstract' symphony and invented the Symphonic Poem, supplying a detailed programme with the score. Later he was joined by Wagner; together they preached the 'synthesis of the arts' which was to have its highest culmination in Wagner's Music Dramas. Schumann wanted no part of this movement. He believed in the Classical ideals of Mozart, Beethoven and Schubert. He resolved to keep the symphony alive. His shining example was Mendelssohn. Soon they would be joined by another master – Brahms. And so the cultural split between Leipzig and Weimar would lead, in the second half of the nineteenth century, to the great 'war of the Romantics', with Brahms and Wagner as the opposing, ideological figureheads. This tremendous conflict all started in Leipzig, and Schumann was at its centre.

The work that best sums up Schumann's achievement during his Leipzig years is his Symphony No. 1 in B flat major (the 'Spring'). It received its première at a Gewandhaus concert, under Mendelssohn's direction, on 31 March 1841.

The Symphony was sketched in the astonishingly short time of four days: from 23 to 26 January 1841. Clara tells us that it was composed mainly at night. A month later, the full score was ready, a *tour de force* of sustained, creative effort. 'It was born in a fiery hour,' Schumann admitted. The four movements originally bore the descriptions, I: Spring's Awakening, II: Evening, III: Merry Playmates, IV: Spring's Farewell. They were later dropped because Schumann felt, significantly, that the listener should not be prejudiced by a title. Still, Schumann himself said (in a letter to Spohr of 23 November 1842) that his chief inspiration was the coming of spring, and the work has been nicknamed the 'Spring' Symphony ever since.

The Introduction opens with an arresting idea on horns and trumpets:

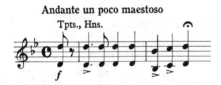

which is immediately taken up by the full orchestra:

Schumann said that he wanted it 'to sound as if from on high, like a call to awaken'. Originally, the Symphony began on B flat:

Schumann overlooked the fact that the old hand horns of the Gewandhaus Orchestra could not play such a passage, and at the first rehearsal
the horn players (who did their best) gave off a sound like a sneeze. The
effect was hilarious, and the orchestra broke up in laughter. Mendelssohn changed the passage to start on D, perfectly possible on a valveless
horn, and that is how the Symphony was published. When Mahler
re-orchestrated the work many years later he restored Schumann's
original idea which makes a great deal of sense thematically, as the
first subject shows.

[Compare with
Schumann's original
opening.]

The slow movement, a simple rondo, contains some of the most telling
orchestral music Schumann had so far composed. Its original title was
'Evening'. Anyone familiar with *Kreisleriana* will have no difficulty in
spotting the allusion to that work which haunts bars 8–11. (See also
page 81.)

The movement ends with a solemn chorale on three trombones:

which has not been heard before, and which is only fully explained when we hear the Scherzo, whose first subject now unfolds a 'thematic transformation' of the chorale.

In a letter to the Berlin conductor Wilhelm Taubert, Schumann once said that he regarded the Finale as 'Spring's Farewell, and that therefore I should not like it to be rendered frivolously'. Its main subject runs:

The metronome mark is Schumann's (see p. 48). The splendid 'echo' effects between first and second violins

remind us of the original seating plan of the Gewandhaus Orchestra, with first violins on the left and second violins on the right. You can hear such passages physically leap from one side of the orchestra to the other, an effect which is often lost through the modern practice of putting all the violins together. In the transition, there is another clear allusion to *Kreisleriana*, this time to that work's closing bars.

To hear Kapellmeister Kreisler stalking through these pages is like unexpectedly spotting an old friend whilst abroad.

81

Altogether, Schumann composed four symphonies. They have never enjoyed the wide following of his piano music. This is strange, since they contain some impressive ideas. Critics, however, point out that he came late to the symphony orchestra, and that his orchestration is sometimes thick and clumsy. Mahler, who was a great Schumann-lover, re-orchestrated all four symphonies, thinning out the textures and transferring certain parts to different instruments, in an effort to make the music 'speak' more clearly. We frequently hear his versions in the concert hall; yet, magnificent though they are, they tell us more about Mahler than about Schumann. In fact, most of the difficulties presented by these symphonies can be resolved by a sympathetic conductor at rehearsal. Today, it is heartening to find among the younger generation of conductors a new respect for Schumann's symphonies which, together with those of Mendelssohn, form the 'missing link' between Beethoven and Brahms.

Schumann did much of his best work during his Leipzig period. If we take a bird's-eye view of his output, a curious characteristic emerges: a tendency to compose works in groups or sets. At first, he had concentrated on piano music. Then in 1840, as we have seen, he had abruptly switched to songs. Now followed two symphonies – the 'Spring' and the D minor which was revised as No. 4. In 1842, he discovered chamber music, writing three string quartets, the Piano Quartet in E flat major, and the famous Piano Quintet in E flat major in swift succession. Later came a spate of choral music, and so on. How can we explain this phenomenon? No other major composer worked quite like it. Schumann had what psychologists call a 'cyclothymic' personality. He liked to exhaust himself in one direction, and then seek relief by exhausting himself in another. Consequently, in both life and art he often seems to be 'stopping and starting' quite arbitrarily. But all that has happened is that the creative impulse has gone underground and re-emerged in a different activity.

To all this composing has to be added, from 1843, Schumann's teaching at the Leipzig Conservatory, to say nothing of the *Neue Zeitschrift* which he ran single-handed and which kept him in continual correspondence with people all over Germany, and beyond. Clara, too, was musically active; apart from her frequent appearances at the Gewandhaus concerts, she undertook two major tours: in 1842 she visited Bremen, Hamburg and Oldenburg, and in 1844 she went as far afield

Schumann

as St. Petersburg where she played before the Russian Imperial Court. On both occasions, as we have seen, Schumann accompanied her.

Schumann suffered two physical breakdowns during this period. The first was in 1842. He put it down to 'overwork', and he and Clara went to relax at the Bohemian spas. The second was much more serious. It began shortly after the Russian tour, in August 1844. The symptoms were ominous. He trembled incessantly, was afflicted by various phobias – such as fear of heights and sharp metallic objects – and, worst of all, he suffered severe aural delusions which made composing impossible. (These symptoms, which until recently baffled Schumann scholars, were first described by Dr. Helbig, the homoeopathic physician at Dresden, whom Schumann consulted in the autumn of 1844. They form part of a much wider clinical picture, and they have to be considered in the light of Schumann's ill health generally, and the disease which first drove him insane and later killed him. The nature of his illness is discussed on p. 117.) In September, Schumann tried to resume his teaching at the Leipzig Conservatory, but his health became worse and he was forced to resign. During some dreadful days in October, while the Schumanns were seeking medical advice in Dresden, Clara, who was at her wits' end, reported that 'Robert did not sleep a single night. His imagination painted the most terrible pictures. In the early morning I generally found him bathed in tears. He gave himself up completely.' Matters were not helped by the arrival of Wieck, who, true to form, attempted to 'rouse him forcibly'.

Convinced that nothing short of a complete change of climate would bring him any benefit, Schumann decided to settle in Dresden permanently. He may have been helped towards this decision by the election of Niels Gade, on the advice of Mendelssohn, to the conductorship of the Gewandhaus concerts in 1844, which Schumann took to be a slight against himself. (In the light of Schumann's disastrous encounter with the Düsseldorf orchestra a few years later, no one could maintain that Mendelssohn had made a mistake.) Within a few weeks, Schumann had severed his connections with Leipzig, including the *Neue Zeitschrift*, whose editorship he now handed over to Lorenz, and after a farewell concert on Sunday 8 December, Robert and Clara left Leipzig for good.

Dresden VII

Whatever illusions the Schumanns cherished about Dresden were soon shattered. Convention ruled all. It was no place for artistic enterprise. Dresden's artistic life was centred around the Royal Court. Here, under the autocratic rule of King Friedrich Augustus II, were gathered painters, sculptors, architects, authors and musicians. Court functions were stifling occasions, governed by rigid protocol; the glittering array of artistic talent which dutifully turned up in support of such events was mostly in the pay of the King, and their liberal outlook stood in bizarre contrast to one of the most reactionary monarchies in Europe. This was an explosive mixture and five years later Dresden was rocked by the 1849 Insurrection. Schumann, who had no direct dealings with the Court, nevertheless chafed under its restrictive influence. At first, he actually savoured the shortage of music. He wrote to Ferdinand David: 'Here one can get back the old lost longing for music, there is so little to hear!' Soon, however, he was completely frustrated by the prevailing spirit of provincialism.

By far the most important musician in Dresden was Richard Wagner, then conductor of the Royal Opera. Schumann was quite unable to appreciate this wayward genius: 'He has the most amazing gift of the gab, and is always chock-full of his own ideas.' Wagner, who could not tolerate Schumann's long silences, was quick to return the compliment: 'He was too conservative to benefit by my views.' As Niecks put it, the unwillingness of the one to unburden himself, and the overwhelming need of the other to do so, created a situation in which, after a few preliminary skirmishes, their relationship slid of its own volition towards a full close. It was an odd situation. Two of the great composers of the day were living within a stone's throw of one another, and the sole extent of their encounter was a few random remarks in each other's literary jottings.

One of Schumann's few musical friends in Dresden was Ferdinand Hiller. He had moved there from Leipzig around 1840 and now directed the Dresden *Liedertafel*, an amateur male-voice choral society. Before long, the two men had joined forces and were attempting to generate some musical activity in Dresden by organizing subscription concerts, like those at the Leipzig Gewandhaus. It was uphill work, and Schumann wrote despairingly to Mendelssohn that the Royal Orchestra was refusing to embark on them, for fear of drawing away the audiences from the long-established pension-fund concerts. A month later, however, he had actually got them started, much to everyone's surprise. Clara, who was billed to take part in the opening concert on 10 November, fell ill; old Wieck (who now lived in Dresden) was despatched post-haste to Leipzig to find a substitute and came back with Joachim, then a mere lad of fourteen, who staggered everybody by playing Mendelssohn's Violin Concerto. This was a promising start. As the concerts got under way, however, Schumann saw that his efforts to bring Dresden up to the level of the Leipzig Gewandhaus were unrealistic; there was a basic lack of interest among the Dresdeners, and after a run of two or three seasons the concerts lapsed.

Clara had little patience with the Dresden musicians. She despised them for their lack of enterprise. She was ruthless in her ambitions for Robert, and doubtless looked back longingly to her concert tours, in the days when she had been able to promote so many of his works. Could she not repeat these early successes? In a mood of determined optimism the Schumanns now arranged a joint visit to Vienna, the scene of one of Clara's greatest triumphs nine years earlier. The couple set out on 24 November 1846. A gloomy reception awaited them. Attendances were thin, the applause was cool, and, worst of all, receipts were down. After the third concert, Robert discovered that they were out of pocket by nearly a hundred ducats. Clara put on a brave face, and wrote euphemistically in her Diary that Robert's music 'took extremely well', and that he 'was recalled several times'. This was wishful thinking. Hanslick, who was in the audience, has left a different account. After the concert he went round to the artists' room, where he found Clara 'complaining bitterly of the coldness and ingratitude of the public. Everything that the rest of us said, endeavouring to soothe her, only increased her vexation. Then Schumann said these never-to-be-forgotten words: "Calm yourself, dear Clara; in ten years' time all this will have changed." ' Disaster now stared them in the face. Their final concert, on 11 January 1847, was still to come. They had to brace themselves to go through with it. Then, out of the blue, Jenny Lind descended on them and offered her services. As the most famous soprano of her time (she was popularly known as the 'Swedish Nightingale') she had a large following wherever she appeared. The last concert, predictably, was sold out. The Schumanns returned to Dresden with a clear profit of 300 thaler. Grateful as they were to Jenny Lind

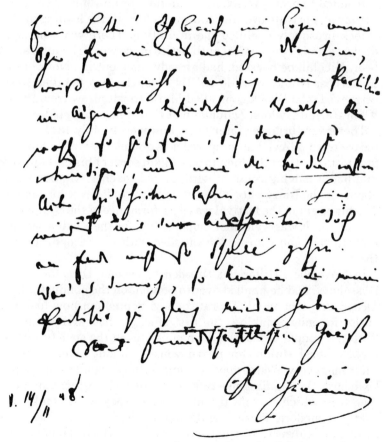

Letter written by Schumann in 1848

it had been a chastening experience. Clara wrote: 'I could not get over the bitter feeling that one song of Lind's had done what I, with all my playing, could not do.'

To make matters worse, old Wieck was now provoking a fresh crop of family quarrels. This time, they centred around his second daughter Marie. For years, Wieck had been grooming her for stardom. He had deliberately (perhaps maliciously) chosen her as Clara's rival and successor. Marie was a competent pianist, but not an outstanding one. With a great fanfare of publicity, Wieck now presented the girl to the world long before she was ready. When Clara and Robert remonstrated, he became abusive. In 1846, while they were in Vienna, the Schumanns attempted to pacify Wieck by arranging for one of his favourite pupils to play at a private evening concert 'before all the leading authorities'. Wieck brusquely declined the invitation. There were, he pompously declared, only two musical authorities in the world: Nicolai and Meyerbeer. Nicolai, he boasted, had already come out in favour of his pupil; Meyerbeer would soon do so! By 1848, the two families were again estranged, and Wieck compelled Marie to withdraw from the Dresden 'Choral Union' which Schumann at that time conducted.

There were brighter interludes, however. In July 1847, Schumann's native town of Zwickau prepared a two-week festival in honour of her greatest son. Here Schumann saw again some of his childhood friends, and had a moving reunion with his old teacher Kuntzsch who went about, as the Diary puts it, 'swelling with pride' over his famous pupil. The highlight of the festival was a performance of the Symphony No. 2, in C major. It was welcome compensation for the Vienna setbacks, and both Robert and Clara were satisfied with the recognition accorded them.

In November, Hiller left Dresden to become Director of Music at Düsseldorf, and he handed over to Schumann the conductorship of the *Liedertafel* – the men's choral society. Schumann now had a regular outlet for music-making, the first since he had arrived in Dresden. Within a couple of months, he had expanded the society into a large-scale 'Choral Union' for mixed voices – about seventy strong. The choir met every Wednesday evening, with Clara accompanying at the keyboard. At the first meeting in January 1848, Schumann made a speech in which he told the new society they would make a special study of modern music, while not neglecting the classics. Under Schumann's direction, they sang music by Bach, Handel and Palestrina, while among contemporary works Mendelssohn's *Athalie*, Hiller's *Geist über dem Wasser* and Schumann's own *Paradise and the Peri* featured in their programmes. Altogether, this was a happy and rewarding activity for Schumann. The society often met for social excursions. There was a particularly memorable outing, one hot summer morning, when they all travelled by steamboat to Meissen and sang in the cathedral; an open-air meal followed in the park, to the singing of quartets, and even a thunderstorm could not quench their enthusiasm. As a direct result of the 'Choral Union', Schumann composed a large number of part-songs; they are among his most neglected compositions, but some of them are well worth reviving today.

Four children were born to the Schumanns during these years: Julie (March, 1845), Emil (February 1846), Ludwig (January 1848), and Ferdinand (July 1849). Clara's hands were now so full (together with her two elder children, Marie and Elise, born in 1841 and 1843, her family leaped from four to eight at Dresden), she had temporarily to abandon her piano-playing.

Schumann himself delighted in his growing family. He always had the happiest relationship with the young. At Dresden, surrounded by his children, he hit upon the idea of composing his famous *Album for the Young* (1848), a collection of forty-four miniatures specially composed for children. Schumann himself described how it all came about.

> I wrote the first pieces as a birthday offering to my eldest daughter and added the others at subsequent intervals.
>
> It seemed to me as if I were once more just beginning to compose, and you will even find traces of my old humour appearing every now and then.
>
> (Letter to Reinecke
> 6 October 1848)

Most young pianists get their first glimpse of greatness in these pieces. There are, as Schumann implies, many examples of humour and even of mock-comedy. But perhaps the piece that Schumann himself preferred above all the others is *Erinnerung* (Remembrance) which he wrote in memory of Mendelssohn who had died the previous year. How fitting (and how original) that one great composer should try to keep alive the memory of another by planting it in the hearts and evergreen minds of the young.

89

Remembrance

Nicht schnell und sehr gesangvoll zu spielen

In 1850, Schumann brought out his celebrated *Advice to Young Musicians*. It is often printed as a preface to *Album for the Young*. Is there a musician anywhere in the world who has not read, and profited from, Schumann's golden words?

'Play always as if a master listened.'
'There is no end to learning.'
'Perhaps it is genius alone that understands genius.'
'By industry and endurance you will always rise higher.'
'Only when the form grows clear to you will the spirit become so too.'

Not one of these aphorisms fails to stimulate thought and provoke discussion.

And the young, in turn, were attracted to Schumann. One story will serve to illustrate the others.

In November 1835, a fourteen-year-old urchin called Alfred Dörffel knocked at Wieck's front door. He desperately wanted to attend a recital Clara was to give in a few days' time, but was too poor to buy a ticket. The door opened, and little Alfchen was led into the drawing-room. There, in the middle of the room, stood the commanding figure of Wieck; Clara and Robert were by the window. Quaking with fright, Alfchen went up to Wieck and the following conversation took place.

'Please sir, I play the piano. I'm studying *Papillons* and I want to go to Clara's concert, but I've got no money.' There was a long silence. Wieck glared at him. 'Put out your hands,' he barked. Alfchen held them out, half expecting a rap on the knuckles. Wieck shook his head at their small span; Alfchen could barely reach a seventh. 'Play for us,' he ordered. The lad sat down at the piano. He had not expected an audition. Frantically, he racked his brains for an excuse.

'This stool is too low for me.' Wieck ignored the remark; he knew how to handle recalcitrant students. 'Begin,' he said imperiously. So Alfchen began. He played *Papillons* – far too quickly. Since he could not manage the octaves, he broke them. The effect was hilarious. Wieck exploded with laughter; Robert and Clara joined in. Alfchen looked puzzled. He always played *Papillons* that way. 'Good,' growled Wieck. 'Be at the stage door. You won't need a ticket.' And on the great evening they gave Alfchen a seat in the front row.

The story of how Alfred Dörffel gate-crashed his first Gewandhaus concert (which he used to tell with relish) became familiar to everybody in Leipzig. Over the years, young Dörffel became a permanent fixture at the Gewandhaus concerts, a kind of mascot, page-turning for such celebrities as Moscheles, Mendelssohn, and Clara herself. He attached himself firmly to the Schumanns and became one of Robert's most ardent disciples. In later life, as a respected musicologist, he wrote a book called *The History of the Gewandhaus Concerts.* How surprised Schumann would have been had he lived to see the title-page of Dörffel's chief work of musical scholarship, which can still be found in the old Peters Edition:

Robert Schumann's
Works
for pianoforte solo
revised by
Alfred Dörffel

It was Dörffel's way of discharging his debt to a master he revered.

Schumann's health now showed signs of further deterioration. His unusual symptoms, first observed in Leipzig (see p. 84), took a disquiet-

Autograph sketch for Papillons, *Op. 2*

ing turn. In May 1846 he had suffered a severe attack of tinnitus (a disturbance of the aural nerve in which the sufferer hears illusory sounds); it made composing impossible. There were ups and downs of mood, too, intense elation alternating with black depression. His fear of heights increased. This last symptom became so marked that by 1850, when he visited Leipzig for a performance of his opera *Genoveva* and was given a bedroom on a high floor, he experienced such terror that he was forced to exchange it for one on the ground level.

These were serious setbacks, and they placed his creative work in perpetual jeopardy. No sooner was he given a respite, starting to revel in his newly-recovered creative strength, than his symptoms broke out again, in Litzmann's phrase, 'as an enemy breaks from an ambush'. Several Schumann scholars, in the light of the great inroads his chronic illness made into his composing, have postulated a 'creative decline'. They see Dresden as a turning-point, and they argue that Schumann never again reached those great expressive peaks depicted in his piano music and his songs. There is a formidable list of compositions, dating from the Dresden years, to challenge their view. Schumann finished his Piano Concerto in A minor, the first performance of which was given by Clara in Leipzig in January 1846; that same year, he completed his Symphony No. 2 in C major. A few months later he began his opera *Genoveva* which occupied him until August 1848; the ink was scarcely dry before he began his incidental music to Byron's *Manfred*, and in the year 1848 he wrote more than twenty works between opp. 67 and 146, including such major compositions as the Concertstück for four horns and orchestra (op. 86) and the Introduction and Allegro Appassionato for piano and orchestra (op. 92). True, these works mark a new stylistic departure; but a stylistic departure is not necessarily a 'creative decline'. It would be unreasonable to expect a composer of Schumann's stature to go on repeating himself.

The undisputed masterpiece of this period is the Piano Concerto in A minor. By common consent it is one of the great Romantic concertos. Schumann had already composed the first movement in 1841, in Leipzig. It was then described as a one-movement *Fantasie* for piano and orchestra. Since he had trouble in placing it with a publisher, however, he shelved it. This was providential. Schumann now revised the *Fantasie*, added two more movements, and there emerged the Concerto with which the whole world has become familiar. Clara gave the first

The title-page for Schumann's cycle, Songs for the Young, *Op. 79*

Schumann

performance of the work at a Leipzig Gewandhaus concert on 1 January 1846.

The Concerto opens with an arresting introduction:

The first subject is given out by the orchestra. It is taken up almost at once by the soloist:

That Schumann was alive to the structural experiments of his day, and to Liszt's 'transformation of themes' technique in particular, is shown by the later uses to which the theme is put. Here is one particularly telling 'transformation' in the Development section; it is now in a major key, and unfolded in augmentation:

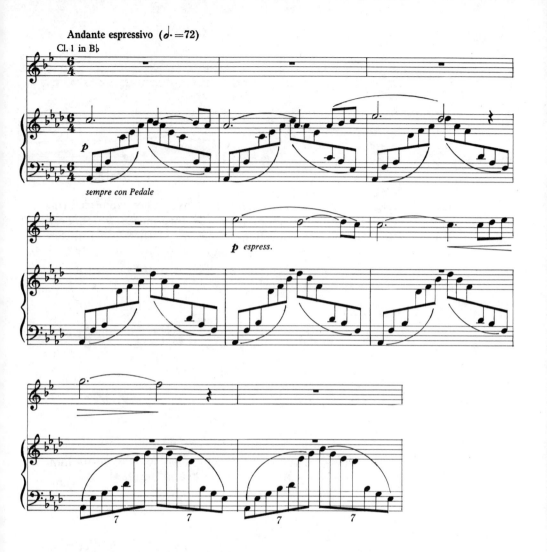

The Cadenza brings home a paramount characteristic of this Concerto. Schumann hated empty virtuosity. He could not abide the 'gladiators of the keyboard', and while he was editor of the *Neue Zeitschrift* he attacked the puffed-up members of the Paris virtuoso school (Herz, Hunten and Pixis, especially) without mercy. And so, when he himself came to write a concerto, it was hardly surprising that he avoided mechanical bravura-work. The Cadenza, in fact, is a sombre piece of imitative counterpoint, based largely on figure 'X' of the main idea:

No one could guess on musical grounds that five years separated the composition of the first movement from the Intermezzo which now follows. Indeed, Schumann establishes a powerful thematic link between the Intermezzo's opening figure and the first movement's first subject. (Compare Figures 'Y', pp. 96 and 98.) It sounds as if the one grew quite naturally out of the other.

The Finale, which flows out of the Intermezzo without a break, contains a famous example of syncopation, quite typical of Schumann. You see the bar-lines in one place, and hear them in another. Is the passage in three-four or three-two time?

Schauffler's comment cannot be bettered: 'Many an orchestral conductor has here met his Waterloo; to the immense (if suppressed) glee of his armed forces.'

During the Dresden period Schumann embarked on an intense and profound study of Bach. For years he had revered Bach as a Titan of musical history. He resented the fact that most of Bach's music remained unpublished, and he now began to press for a complete edition of the master's works. The carrying out of this vast project was begun in 1850, the centenary of Bach's death, by the *Bachgesellschaft* ('Bach Society of Friends') and Schumann played a major role in getting it all started. On 24 April 1845, a pedal-board was delivered to Schumann's house and attached beneath his piano. He could now practise Bach's organ works. Among the unusual compositions he wrote for the 'pedal-piano' are his *Six Fugues on the name Bach*, op. 60. 'This,' said Schumann, 'is a composition at which I worked for a whole year in order that I might make it worthy of the great name it bears, and which I believe will outlive all my others.' In the last part of that statement he was mistaken. None the less, the 'BACH' fugues reveal considerable craftsmanship in their grasp of strict counterpoint, which Schumann, ever since his early theoretical studies with Dorn, had never found easy. $\longrightarrow$

In May 1849, the Dresden Insurrection broke out. Barricades were flung up (built to specifications drawn up by Wagner!) and bitter hand-to-hand fighting ensued. Twenty-six fleeing students, found hidden in a single room, were taken out one by one and shot. Dozens of people were thrown out of fourth-storey windows, their bodies broken on the cobblestones below. Liberal though he was, Schumann had no stomach for violence. The sight of fourteen corpses laid out in the courtyard of the local Clinic revolted him. Nor could he face the thought of compulsory enlistment. Twice the 'press gangs' came knocking at his door, and twice Clara emphatically denied that he was in. When they threatened to search the house, Schumann fled through the back garden with Clara and his eldest daughter Marie, and stayed with friends at the nearby village of Maxen. Clara showed immense courage by going back the following day, risking the street firing and the patrolling soldiers, in order to pick up the younger children whom she had left in the house and now found asleep in bed. The Schumanns sought temporary sanctuary in the tiny village of Kreischa, and here Robert withdrew from horrible reality and buried himself in composition.

Fugue I

Throughout 1849, Schumann's desire for a regular position in the world of music increased. Clara, too, was impatient on his behalf. She longed for him to gain an official post in keeping with his growing status as a composer. In 1847, doubtless as a result of her prodding, he had inquired after the directorship of the Vienna Conservatory which had fallen vacant. Again, shortly after the death of Mendelssohn, he had put out discreet feelers about the conductorship of the Gewandhaus Orchestra. Although these moves came to nothing, they indicated his underlying dissatisfaction. When, in the autumn of 1849, he received a

100

letter from his old friend Hiller, about to take up a new appointment at Cologne and offering Schumann the music directorship of Düsseldorf, he decided to accept. The decision was complicated for him by a curious discovery.

> The other day I looked for some notices of Düsseldorf in an old geography book, and among the places of note in that town I found mentioned three convents and a mad-house. I have no objection to the former, but it made me quite uncomfortable to read about the latter. I will tell you how that is: a few years ago, as you will remember, we lived at Maxen. I there discovered that the principal view from my windows was on to the Sonnenstein. At last I perfectly hated the sight of it, and it entirely spoilt my stay there. So I thought the same thing might happen at Düsseldorf. But possibly the notice is altogether incorrect, and the institution may be merely a hospital, such as one finds in every town.

Later events give his morbid observations tragic overtones. Clara, however, was more down-to-earth. She was firmly resolved they should leave Dresden, a town she had come to detest. After fulfilling a round of concert engagements in Bremen, Hamburg and Altona, the Schumanns finally set out for Düsseldorf on 1 September 1850.

Schumann, 1850

VIII   *Düsseldorf and the End*

Düsseldorf was a garden city. It possessed broad, leafy avenues and shady walks, which lent it an air of quiet distinction. The Rhine flowed past it, on its eight-hundred-mile journey across Germany, and watered some of its public grounds. The houses were large and spacious. They were built by the wealthy manufacturers who lived there, people who would shortly destroy the rustic character of Düsseldorf with their heavy industries. To the west, and just outside the city, were wooded hills, dotted here and there with restaurants, the popular haunts of local artists. In the city itself was the beautiful Hofgarten, with its mirror-pond and bridge. Schumann could often be seen walking there. Niecks, as a boy, well remembered catching sight of him with an absorbed expression on his face, his lips characteristically pursed as in a silent whistle. Schumann loved the Rhineland, and he identified with his new surroundings at once.

From the start, Robert and Clara were given a warm welcome. The Düsseldorfers, anxious to please their new Director and his distinguished pianist wife, had laid on an enthusiastic reception for them. The couple were met by a deputation of concert officials, led by Hiller, and escorted to the best hotel in town, where comfortable rooms, decked out with flowers, had been placed at their disposal. Later that evening, they were serenaded by the choir. Next day, while dining in the hotel, they heard the strains of Mozart's *Don Giovanni* Overture coming from the next room, played by a contingent from the town orchestra. 'It was a most pleasing surprise to Robert,' Clara wrote in her Diary. 'They played everything well, and I think Robert will be able to do something with the orchestra.' Her words have a hollow ring in the light of subsequent events.

102   Schumann's duties at Düsseldorf were quite simple. He was to direct

Clara Schumann, 1859

the public subscription concerts throughout each season. The forces at his disposal consisted, first and foremost, of the large chorus. There were 120 singers, and Schumann was expected to rehearse them once a week. They were all amateurs, but under Hiller they had reached a high standard of excellence. The orchestra, on the other hand, was a professional body, and rehearsals were less frequent. Additionally, Schumann was expected to fulfil certain obligations towards the local Catholic church services whenever large musical forces were required. The first concert of the season was on 24 October. A few days earlier, Schumann had appointed Wasielewski (his former pupil and first biographer) as the new orchestral leader, for he was determined to maintain a high level of performance. There was a large audience present, and as Schumann mounted the rostrum he was greeted with a triple fanfare. The programme included Beethoven's 'Consecration of the House' Overture, and Mendelssohn's G minor Piano Concerto, with Clara as soloist. Everybody agreed that the concert was an unqualified success, and Schumann had good reason to feel pleased.   103

Why, then, did relations between him and the orchestra sink to such a low level that, within a couple of years, the latter were demanding his resignation? It is a long and harrowing story.

Schumann was not a conductor. That fact needs to be stressed. He had neither the training nor the temperament for it. At first, he commanded respect among the players by virtue of his reputation in the wider world of music; but at Düsseldorf that reputation wore thin. His baton technique was non-existent. He lacked the capacity to express himself clearly and concisely at rehearsals. Moreover, he indulged in the tiresome habit of repeating passages many times without telling the orchestra why he was doing so. There was no quicker way of killing enthusiasm. Even Joachim, one of Schumann's most loyal friends, could find no good in him on the rostrum:

> In earlier days he may have beaten time accurately enough, but he made no remarks on the performances. At the rehearsal of *Paradise and the Peri* Clara (at the piano) said: 'My husband says that he wishes this passage *piano*'; and he stood by and nodded gratefully. If it did not go well, moral indignation. At a performance of one of his own symphonies he stood dreamily with raised baton, all the players ready and not knowing when to begin. Königslöw and I, who sat at the first desk, therefore took the matter into our own hands and began, Schumann following with a smile of pleasure.

This is such strange behaviour that it makes no sense to interpret it, as Schumann's colleagues did, as simple incompetence. There were many bizarre scenes arising from Schumann's attempts to conduct, and some of them attracted a lot of publicity. We shall only come to understand them when we view them against the wider context of his illness, which slowly encroached on all his activities and rendered him increasingly uncoordinated in his movements, his speech, his hearing.

Not surprisingly, discipline began to flag; some of the chorus became bored and stayed away from rehearsals. Schumann, oddly oblivious to his own faults, interpreted their action as a personal slight. But the first hint of real trouble came at the end of the season. The local newspaper published an anonymous article attacking his capacity for leadership. Schumann was outraged. He believed the writer to be a member of his own Concerts Committee, and suspected a plot. Clara fumed into her Diary: 'It is a disgrace that they should quietly acquiesce in such treatment of Robert at the hands of the Düsseldorfers, instead of shielding him in every way as they should do, in order to keep him.' Clara was, in fact, the one person who might have saved the situation. She could tactfully have helped Schumann towards a more objective understanding of his function as a conductor. But her blind devotion to her husband left her utterly incapable of accepting any criticism of him, let alone offering it; and so he lurched from one crisis to another.

The next two seasons produced a whole crop of embarrassing situations. Once, at choir practice, the sopranos were singing several high As. The effect caused such merriment within their ranks that they stopped singing, and the performance just petered out. Schumann noticed nothing and went on conducting. Tausch, his assistant, who was accompanying, continued playing for a few bars and then decided that he, too, had better stop. Schumann beckoned him to the rostrum. Instead of offering a reproof, Schumann merely pointed to a bar in the full score and murmured: 'See, this bar is beautiful!' On another occasion, during Mass, he continued conducting after the music had stopped and the priest had started to intone. Observers said that it was as if he had withdrawn from reality and was conducting some inner performance of the music.

There were humorous sides to the situation, however. He frequently dropped his baton. Niecks remembers his father (who was one of Schumann's orchestral players) telling him that once, after this happened at rehearsal, Schumann came up to him with his baton tied to his wrist with a piece of string, and exclaimed gaily: 'Look, now it can't fall again!' This curious anecdote is related by Niecks without comment. An obvious explanation as to why Schumann kept dropping his baton is that he had a crippled right hand, and grasped objects with difficulty. His hand injury must have invaded every subsequent activity Schumann engaged in. Litzmann, for instance, mentions his notoriously illegible handwriting, and also offers no comment. With one finger straddled across the others (Schumann's description) what else was to be expected?

Among the works Schumann composed during this difficult period was his Cello Concerto in A minor, op. 129. It was completed in the remarkably short space of two weeks. The piece displays some unusual features. Its three contrasting movements are rolled into one to make a continuously unfolding composition of thirty minutes. Again, the

105

soloist's cadenza, which occurs in the *last* movement (an original stroke, this) is accompanied. (Did Elgar take this as the model for his Violin Concerto, where the same thing happens in the same spot?) Finally, the Concerto is a 'cyclic' work, quoting one or two of its own themes across movements.

The impassioned principal subject, with which the Concerto begins, is typical of the melodic invention Schumann poured into the work.

Why Schumann wrote a cello concerto at all remains something of a mystery. In his day, the cello had hardly begun to emerge as a concerto instrument. Perhaps there was an element of nostalgia involved. We know that Schumann played the cello in his youth. After the injury to his right hand he wrote to his mother from Leipzig on 6 November 1832: 'I am for my part completely resigned. . . . In Zwickau I will take up the violoncello again (for which only the left hand is needed) which besides is very useful for symphonic compositions. . . .'

The Concerto remained unperformed during Schumann's lifetime. It had to wait until 1860 before it was given its première in Leipzig, with Ludwig Ebert as soloist.

Another work dating from the Düsseldorf period is the Symphony in E flat major (the 'Rhenish'). On 29 September 1850, Robert and Clara had travelled down the Rhine to Cologne. The river journey, with its splendid views of the Seven Hills, enchanted them. But what impressed Robert most was the majestic sight of Cologne Cathedral, a supreme piece of Gothic architecture. He returned to Düsseldorf with the inspiration for a new five-movement symphony which would reflect the life of his beloved Rhine – its scenery, its legends, its pageantry, the industrious character of its peoples. Two of its movements, in fact, originally bore descriptive titles. The Scherzo was called 'Morning on the Rhine'; while the solemn fourth movement, directly inspired by Cologne Cathedral and the ceremonials surrounding the elevation of Archbishop von Geissel to the Cardinalate, was described as 'In the style of an accompaniment to a solemn ceremony.' Schumann later dropped these titles. As he put it: 'One should not show one's heart to the public.' The first performance took place in Düsseldorf on 6 February 1851, with Schumann conducting. It was instantly successful. Within a month it had received three performances. Simrock published it the same year.

The 'Rhenish' Symphony opens with this soaring theme:

Its metrical displacements are highly characteristic of Schumann.

Like the Finale of the Piano Concerto (p. 98), you see the bar-lines in one place and hear them in another.

The awe which was inspired in Schumann by Cologne Cathedral found its full expression in the solemn music of the fourth movement. Tovey described it as 'one of the finest pieces of ecclesiastical polyphony since Bach'. It begins with a sombre idea on horns and trombones:

Later, this idea is transformed and worked out in a highly elaborate piece of imitative counterpoint, based on figure 'X'.

Schumann allows us to hear fleeting references to 'X' in the brisk Finale

like glimpses of a distant cathedral spire flashing in the setting sun.

By the winter of 1852, Schumann's troubles with the Orchestral Committee had become chronic. Dissatisfied with his leadership, they wrote a stiff letter to Schumann, criticizing his handling of the rehearsals. They implied he should resign. He refused, so the Committee resigned instead. A new Committee was-formed. This time they suc-ceeded in persuading Schumann to hand over the choir rehearsals to Tausch, while retaining the direction of the orchestra and public concerts himself. This arrangement came into force at the beginning of 1853. It was an uneasy truce. Bad feeling had been aroused on both sides. It required only one major artistic indiscretion on Schumann's part to bring matters to a head, and he quickly provided it. On 16 October he conducted a mass by Hauptmann in St. Maximilian's Church. The performance was so bad, the conducting so apathetic, that the public accused the musicians of lacking respect for the Holy Office. Less than two weeks later, Schumann once again led his forces to the brink of disaster. This time, it was a public concert. Joachim was the visiting soloist, and his name had drawn a large audience. Schumann's conducting was incoherent; he was quite unable to start the performance and stood with his arms raised, waiting for the players to commence. Eventually, they did so; but they followed Joachim, not Schumann, who was left to grope his way along as best he could. It was the last occasion Schumann ever conducted in Düsseldorf. The Committee insisted that he hand over the remaining concerts to Tausch. On 10 November the Schumanns thankfully left Düsseldorf for a con-cert tour of Holland. They were glad to get away, if only for a few weeks. It was the most humiliating episode of Schumann's career.

It is easy to blame the long-suffering Düsseldorfers. Was not Schu-mann one of the great composers of his time? And by his immense prestige had he not brought honour to Düsseldorf? That was Clara's view precisely. The Düsseldorfers had only one reply: they had had nothing to do with Schumann's appointment. They had accepted him simply because Hiller, their outgoing Director, had recommended him. In the event, Schumann had proved inadequate to the task. Were they now expected to sit back silently and suffer the consequences? More-over, there is clear evidence that Schumann had already entered the final stages of his fatal illness, and was hardly fit enough to fulfil his duties. The symptoms were ominous. In June 1851 he had suffered a series of 'nervous attacks', as he called them. Clara was more specific. She recorded in her Diary that terrible morning in July 1853 when Schumann got up and was seized by a paralytic stroke. His speech disorder, which made his pronunciation sound clumsy and indistinct, dates from this period.

109

The one shaft of light which brightened an otherwise dark year was the coming of Brahms. Towards the end of September 1853, at the height of Schumann's troubles with the Committee, the twenty-year-old Brahms appeared, bearing a letter of introduction from Joachim. It was one of the great moments of musical history. Brahms sat down at the piano and started playing one of his piano sonatas. He had progressed no farther than a few bars when Schumann, electrified, rushed out of the room and came back dragging Clara behind him. 'Now, my dear Clara,' he said, 'you will hear such music as you never heard before; and you, young man, play the work from the beginning.' The meeting was to have fateful consequences for all three musicians. Brahms stayed with the Schumanns throughout the month of October, becoming one of Robert's most devoted disciples. Schumann referred to him as 'the young eagle'. He wrote to Breitkopf and Härtel on the young man's behalf, insisting that they take up his music. The extent to which Brahms modelled himself on Schumann has never been fully chronicled. There are some telling examples showing the bearing of the older master on the younger one. In the slow movement of Schumann's 'Spring' Symphony, for instance, there occurs the following passage:

Larghetto

Is this not the model on which the first subject of Brahms's F major Symphony is based?

Again, taking the opening subject of Schumann's C major Symphony:

Allegro ma non troppo

Does this idea not lurk behind Brahms's Violin Concerto?

Allegro non troppo

It was while Brahms was staying with the Schumanns that the famous tribute to Joachim was planned. Joachim, one of the great violinists of the day, was about to visit Düsseldorf. Why not present him with a new violin sonata? Brahms and Schumann got to work enthusiastically, and brought in Albert Dietrich (a pupil of Schumann's) to speed things up. The result was the so-called 'F.A.E.' Sonata; Schumann wrote the slow movement and the finale, leaving the Scherzo to Brahms and the first movement to Dietrich. The nickname derives from Joachim's personal motto: *Frei aber einsam* 'free but solitary'. From time to time, you can hear Joachim's motto speak quite clearly.

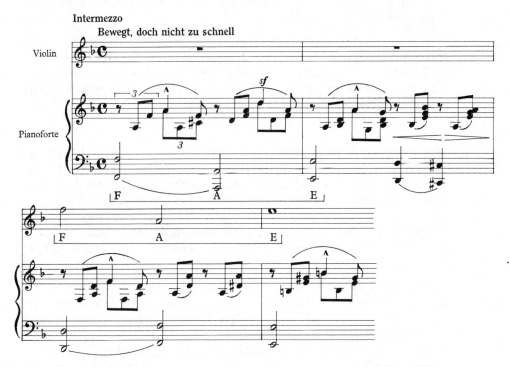

Joachim, incidentally, on being presented with this unusual gift, was asked to identify each 'anonymous' composer in turn, which he did very easily. The final outcome of this encounter between Brahms and Schumann was Schumann's famous article 'New Paths', published in the *Zeitschrift*, in which he hailed Brahms as a genius. Schumann

111

reminded his readers that it was ten years since he had contributed to his old magazine, and that 'many new and significant talents' had emerged in the meantime – Joachim, Gade, Heller, Dietrich. He went on:

> It seemed to me, who followed the progress of these chosen ones with the greatest interest, that . . . a musician would inevitably appear to whom it was vouchsafed to give the highest and most ideal expression to the tendencies of our time, one who would not show his mastery in a gradual development, but, like Athena, would spring fully armed from the head of Zeus. And he has come, a young man over whose cradle Graces and Heroes stood watch. His name is Johannes Brahms.

This was lavish praise to bestow on an unknown, twenty-year-old composer. Overnight, it launched Brahms to fame. Brahms was deeply appreciative. He remained a steadfast and loyal friend to Schumann throughout his days of dark despair, now almost upon him, and he provided solace and comfort for Clara in her hour of need.

On the night of 10 February 1854, Schumann reported a 'very strong and painful aural affection'. Four days later, on 14 February, he was sitting in a restaurant with his friend Becker, the violinist. He put down his newspaper and said: 'I can't read any more. I keep hearing the note A.' The aural illusions progressed, and Schumann recorded hearing 'magnificent music, with instruments of splendid resonance, the like of which has never been heard on earth before.' Clara wrote in her Diary:

> My poor Robert suffers terribly. All sounds are transformed for him into music. . . . He has said several times that if it does not stop he'll go out of his mind. . . . The trouble with his ears has now got to the point of his hearing great symphonic pieces played right through with the last note held until another piece comes into his imagination.

During the night of the 17th, Schumann experienced a dramatic visual hallucination. He claimed that angels were with him. He got out of bed and took down a tune in E flat major which, he said, the angels had dictated to him:

Moderato

The tune bears a striking resemblance to the slow movement of Schumann's own Violin Concerto composed the previous year. Schumann later wrote a set of variations on it (so, too, did Brahms) which were only published in 1939.

On the 18th the 'angels' were transformed into devils, appearing in the form of tigers and hyenas. Two doctors were summoned. One of them was Dr. Hasenclaver, the family physician; he immediately brought in an army doctor, Dr. Böger, and they examined Schumann together. Clara was a witness to that dreadful day.

> His condition soon became hysterical. He cried out in agony, and
> the two doctors, who luckily were there, could hardly hold him.
> I shall never forget the way he looked at me; I suffered with him
> the most cruel torments. After about half an hour he calmed down
> and said that the friendly voices were making themselves heard
> again and giving him back his courage. The doctors got him to bed.

Sunday 19 February was a distressing day. Schumann claimed to be surrounded by evil spirits, 'those superterrestrial and subterranean men', as he called them, and they persecuted him until nightfall. The following day, he was overcome by feelings of guilt and remorse; he kept repeating that he was a criminal, that he would go to Hell, and that he must never stop reading the Bible. On 26 February he asked to be taken to a lunatic asylum; he feared doing his wife and children an injury. He ate his evening meal in great haste, and went to gather all the things he might require for his journey. Clara and Hasenclaver persuaded him to go to bed instead. Next day, while Clara was preoccupied, Schumann left the house in the pouring rain, wearing only his dressing-gown and slippers, went straight to the Rhine Bridge, climbed on to a parapet, and threw himself into the river. Just before he plunged, he removed his wedding ring and cast it into the Rhine. (A note was later found in his bedroom. 'Dear Clara: I shall cast my wedding ring into the Rhine. Do you do the same. Then the two rings will be united.' Oddly, this action fulfilled a dream Schumann had had   113 sixteen years earlier, in November 1837, during the turbulent days of his courtship, in which he said he cast his engagement ring into a deep pool.) As he fell, he was spotted by some fishermen, and was dragged out of the whirling current, half dead; he is said to have made a second attempt from the boat. He was forcibly carried home. Marie Schumann, his eldest daughter, has left this moving account of the tragedy. She was thirteen years old.

> I saw my father for the last time the day he went out to take his life. . . . My mother had to talk to the doctor, and I was to stay in the little room and see if my father in the next room wanted anything. I had been standing for a moment in front of my mother's bureau when the door between the two rooms opened and my father appeared in the doorway in his long green-flowered dressing-gown. He was dreadfully pale. Seeing me, he hid his face in his hands, and said: 'Oh, My God!' Then he disappeared again. I stood for a minute rooted to the spot; then, remembering why I was there, I went into my father's room. It was empty; and the door to my parents' bedroom, and the one beyond that to the hall, were both wide open. I rushed in to my mother. The doctor was still there, and we searched all the rooms. It was obvious my father had gone out. We tried to find him, my mother telling me to go to Fräulein Leser's to tell her what had happened. In the street I saw people coming towards me talking loudly, and when I was nearer I recognized my father. Two men were holding him up under the armpits, while he held his hands in front of his face.

Clara, on the verge of collapse, was not allowed to see him. She was not even told of the suicide attempt. (It was only after Schumann's death, two years later, that she learned the truth when she asked for his missing wedding ring.) Two male nurses were brought in to look after the sick composer. He again requested to be sent to an asylum, and this time Dr. Hasenclaver complied. Arrangements were made for him to be taken to the private asylum of Dr. Richarz at Endenich, near Bonn. The carriage called for him on 4 March and Schumann, apparently in a state of euphoria, and without so much as a farewell to his wife and children, left home for good.

Schumann spent the next two years at Endenich. He thought he would be cured there. That was not to be. His illness slowly increased its hold over him. He would pace the floor of his room incessantly and frequently kneel down and wring his hands. Sometimes, he held imaginary conversations with voices which denounced his compositions as plagiarisms. He would then become agitated and exclaim aloud: 'That's not true! That is a lie!' Quite frequently he refused to eat, and towards the end of his illness he became emaciated. According to Brahms, who visited him on 14 August 1854, he had suddenly stopped drinking his wine the day before, complaining that it had been poisoned, and he poured the rest of it on the floor.

He was not incarcerated. Dr. Richarz's asylum stood in spacious gardens surrounded by trees and Schumann was free to wander back

Front, l. to r.
Ludwig, Felix,
Ferdinand,
Eugenie;
back
Marie, Elise

The children of Robert and Clara Schumann, c. 1855

and forth at will. He made frequent pilgrimages to Beethoven's monument in near-by Bonn, and in his room he had a piano, manuscript paper, and writing utensils, so that he was able to compose.

Throughout 1855 Schumann's condition steadily worsened. Brahms visited him for a second time in February 1855 and noted chronic memory failure, accompanied by a violent insistence on the reliability of his recollections whenever they were doubted. A few months later, in the summer of 1855, Schumann's biographer Wasielewski watched him, unobserved, extemporizing at the piano, and described him unforgettably 'like a machine whose springs are broken, but which still tries to work, jerking convulsively'. By the autumn of 1855 Dr. Richarz had given up all hope of recovery. Brahms was one of the last persons to see him alive. He travelled to Endenich in June 1856. Schumann was confined to bed with swollen feet. What lingered in Brahms's memory was the sight of Schumann picking names from an atlas and grouping them in strict alphabetical order. His old obsession with word-play had remained to the end. On 23 July Clara received a telegram from Dr. Richarz: 'If you want to see your husband alive, come with all haste.' Clara saw Schumann for the first time in over two years on Sunday 27 July, 'between six and seven in the evening. He smiled at me, and with great exertion – for he could no longer control his limbs – put his arm about me. I shall never forget it. Not all the treasures in the world could equal this embrace.'

The following day, Clara helped him to take a little wine. Some of it spilt over her hand and Schumann, 'with the happiest expression and real haste', licked it from her fingers. Throughout the 28th his limbs were in almost continuous convulsions. He died the next day, Tuesday 29 July, at four o'clock in the afternoon. Two days later he was buried in Bonn. Brahms, Joachim and Dietrich, his youthful admirers, were the honorary pallbearers, and Grillparzer delivered an oration at the graveside. The only other people present at the funeral, apart from Clara, were Hiller and members of the *Concordiagesellschaft* who had serenaded Robert's arrival in Düsseldorf six years earlier.

The true nature of Schumann's illness was regarded as a mystery by the medical profession for nearly a century. No single diagnosis accounted for all the symptoms. In 1873 Dr. Richarz first aroused interest in the problem when he published his autopsy findings. (His report appeared in an Appendix to Wasielewski's biography of

Schumann.) The brain was removed and examined; its weight was below normal for a man of Schumann's age. Richarz finally diagnosed 'general paresis' – a partial paralysis of the muscles which does not affect sensation. Unfortunately, it was impossible to check Richarz's findings, as the hospital notes relating to Schumann's case mysteriously disappeared from Endenich shortly afterwards. Möbius, in his foundation work on Schumann's illness, suggested that Richarz himself had removed them; he concluded that Schumann had suffered a series of schizophrenic attacks from early manhood onwards. This diagnosis provoked wide disagreement from other authorities. Over the years, in fact, Schumann has turned up frequently in the medical journals and has been saddled with a variety of terminal illnesses, ranging from tubercular meningitis to a tumour on the brain. Meanwhile, Schumann's biographers have hovered uncertainly over the various choices offered them.

In 1959, the mystery was solved. Dr. Eliot Slater and Dr. Alfred Meyer (specialists in the fields of psychiatry and neuropathology respectively) published a joint paper in which they reviewed all the medical evidence and asserted that the only disease to fit all the facts was tertiary syphilis. Is it possible that Richarz himself, who, after all, observed Schumann daily for two years or more, suspected this disease and suppressed the hospital records to spare Clara further humiliation? We shall never know. Only one thing is certain. Schumann must have contracted the disease fairly early, since one or two of the symptoms on which the diagnosis is based appeared at least twelve years before he died. As early as 1844, for instance, Schumann had complained of 'singing noises' in the ears – a classic symptom of secondary syphilis. Considering the long latency period required if the disease is to run its natural course, the most likely time of infection was 1830–1 during his boisterous days as a student in Leipzig. This is borne out by the newly published *Tagebücher* (1973) in which Schumann chronicles his encounters with the opposite sex in extraordinary detail.

And what of Clara? During her sixteen-year marriage to Schumann, her lot was not particularly rosy. She was obliged, by her circumstances, to suppress her own career in favour of her husband's; she bore him eight children; finally, she took the full brunt of his tragic illness until he was placed in the Endenich asylum, two years before the end. After Robert's death, she courageously gathered together the threads of her former career and made a fresh start. She was still only thirty-six years

117

Schumann in silhouette

old. Eventually, she moved with her young family to Berlin, where she stayed with her mother (who, it will be remembered, had meanwhile married the musician Adolf Bargiel). From 1863, she adopted Baden-Baden as her headquarters, her foreign concert tours gradually taking up more of her time. During this period of intensive concert-giving, Clara gradually built up a reputation as the greatest woman pianist of her day. Her restraint at the keyboard, and her fidelity to the text, were unusual at a time when the bravura pianist was enjoying his hey-day. Hanslick heard her often, and wrote: 'She could be called the greatest living pianist, rather than the greatest female pianist, were the range of her physical strength not limited by her sex. . . . Everything is distinct, clear, sharp as a pencil sketch.' She never lost an opportunity of playing Schumann's music, and her interpretations came to be regarded as authoritative. For many years she appeared regularly in London, the last occasion being in 1888. From 1878 she was principal piano professor at the Frankfurt am Main Conservatory of Music. She died in 1896, aged seventy-seven, and was laid to rest in Robert's grave in Bonn.

Schumann's Family Tree

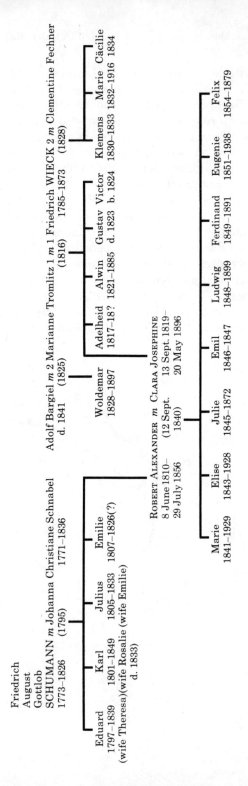

Schumann's family is indicated on the left; Clara Wieck's is indicated on the right.

The inter-relationship of their families was complicated by Friedrich Wieck's two marriages. His first marriage, to Marianne Tromlitz, produced five children: Adelheid, Clara, Alwin, Gustav and Victor. After its dissolution, in 1824, Wieck eventually contracted a second marriage, in 1828, to Clementine Fechner, which produced three more children: Klemens, Marie and Cäcilie. Meanwhile, Wieck's first wife married Adolf Bargiel and had by him a son, the composer Woldemar Bargiel. Thus, Clara's childhood must have been confusing for her. She had Alwin, Victor, and Gustav Wieck as brothers; she had Klemens, Marie and Cäcilie as halfbrother and halfsisters; and she had Woldemar as a halfbrother.

Suggestions for Further Reading

The definitive biography of Schumann has not yet been written. Such a statement, made about one of the great composers of history, sounds implausible; indeed, until recently it could not have been made. Schumann scholars had every reason to suppose that they were familiar with all the significant details of his life and work. That is no longer the case. A new crop of discoveries has been made which throws fresh light on both the man and his music. His finger injury, his terminal illness, his 'faulty' metronome, his use of verbal imagery in composing – all these areas have yielded new information which is at present available only in learned journals and foreign archives, and which is still waiting to be written into an authoritative narrative. Meanwhile, the most effective books on Schumann are those of the 'documentary' type, based on his own correspondence, his Diary entries, and his impressive literary output.

One of the most informative books on Schumann ever to appear is by Frederick Niecks: *Robert Schumann, a Supplementary and Corrective Biography*. Although it was written in 1924, and is not free from error, it remains a foundation-work on the composer. Niecks was on terms of intimate friendship with many of the leading personalities who played a role in Schumann's life. In 1889, he interviewed several people in connection with his Schumann biography, including Dorn (Schumann's old theory teacher) and Clara Schumann herself, which produced basic material to which all subsequent books on Schumann are indebted.

Undoubtedly, the most monumental book in the Schumann literature is Berthold Litzmann's *Clara Schumann: An Artist's Life* which appeared during the years 1902–8 in three volumes. Litzmann had access to the Schumann Diaries, and to a vast amount of unpublished correspondence. The central character is Clara, but for much of the

121

time Schumann himself dominates these pages. The result is an impeccable piece of Schumann scholarship, mandatory reading for anyone who wishes to come to grips with Schumann's life. Litzmann's work was abridged and translated into English in 1913.

Among the shorter biographies which are still readily available, two can be recommended for their readability and for their sympathetic treatment of the composer: *Florestan: the Life and Work of Robert Schumann,* by Robert Schauffler, and *Schumann* (Master Musician Series) by Joan Chissell.

Summary of Schumann's Works

Piano
Three Sonatas
Thirteen 'Suites' (including *Papillons*, *Carnaval*, *Kreisleriana*, *Faschingsschwank*, and *Scenes of Childhood*).
Twelve Concert Studies (2 vols.) after Paganini Caprices
Variations (including '*Abegg*' and *Études Symphoniques*)
Fantasie in C major
Miscellaneous works (including *Humoreske* and *Arabeske*)

Songs
Three hundred Songs, at least, including the Song Cycles *Dichterliebe* (Heine), *Frauenliebe und -leben* (Chamisso), *Liederkreis*, op. 24, (Eichendorff), and *Myrthen* (miscellaneous poets)

Chamber Music
Three String Quartets
Three Violin and Piano Sonatas
Three Piano Trios
One Piano Quintet
One Piano Quartet

Orchestral
Four Symphonies
Five Overtures
Three Concertos (for piano, cello, and violin respectively)

Choral Music

About one hundred choral compositions and part-songs for accompanied, and unaccompanied voices, including *Paradise and the Peri* and *Scenes from Goethe's 'Faust'*

Opera and Theatre Music

Genoveva (opera)
Manfred (incidental music)

Literary Works

Schumann's literary output was vast. For ten years (1834–44), as editor of the *Neue Zeitschrift*, he produced a steady stream of articles, criticisms, and letters which fill many volumes.

Of the many selections which have been edited and translated for the English reader, one of the best is *The Musical World of Robert Schumann* by Henry Pleasants.

Index